Delos Franklin Wilcox

Study of City Government

An outline of the problems of municipal functions, control and organization

Delos Franklin Wilcox

Study of City Government
An outline of the problems of municipal functions, control and organization

ISBN/EAN: 9783337312763

Printed in Europe, USA, Canada, Australia, Japan

Cover: Foto ©Suzi / pixelio.de

More available books at **www.hansebooks.com**

THE STUDY

OF

CITY GOVERNMENT

AN OUTLINE OF

THE PROBLEMS OF MUNICIPAL FUNCTIONS
CONTROL AND ORGANIZATION

BY

DELOS F. WILCOX, A.M., Ph.D.

New York
THE MACMILLAN COMPANY
LONDON: MACMILLAN & CO., Ltd.
1897

All rights reserved

COPYRIGHT, 1897,
BY THE MACMILLAN COMPANY.

Norwood Press
J. S. Cushing & Co. — Berwick & Smith
Norwood Mass. U.S.A.

AUTHOR'S PREFACE

This little book now offered to the public has taken its present form rather sooner than was at first intended. It is the outgrowth of a bare outline or scheme of the problems of city government, prepared during the past year in connection with private tutoring work. In spite of the recent increased interest in municipal affairs, many people ask, when a student of city government announces himself, "Why! what is there in that to study?" The outline which forms the basis of this volume was prepared in order to show people just what there is in city government that it is worth while to study. After having written out the scheme of the problems of municipal functions, control, and organization, with a few introductory and concluding remarks, I began to illustrate the matters contained therein by notes referring to authorities, to the experience of various cities, and to points of controversy in public law and political science. After the notes had been completed they were more than twice as bulky as the original text. When the question of publication came to be seriously considered, I was straightway advised to incorporate most of the notes in the text itself. This I have done, though with some reluctance. In this way the character of the work has been changed from that of an illustrated outline of problems to that of a general treatise. I had intended, after a few years more of careful study and thought upon the problems of city government, to expand the outline into a fairly comprehensive treatise of the whole subject. With my present knowledge I have not been able to do this. The result is that a little book is now presented which is primarily an outline of problems, but which also contains some discussion and many illustrations. The variety of forms and functions of city government is so great, and complete information is so difficult to obtain, that I have been unable to treat any item of any problem exhaustively. This fact must be constantly borne in mind by the reader of these pages. For example, I was not aware, until after the chapter on the problems of function had taken final shape, that the corporation of the city of Glasgow supports nine churches to this day, and appoints a representative elder as a member of the General Assembly of the Church of Scotland.

The problem of the city is so intense and so unlimited that every intelligent citizen who has given no attention to municipal problems owes an apology to his country and to his race. And the student who aspires to be a scholar can devote himself to no richer or inspiring field than the modern city, its government, its institutions, and its tendencies. As government is the most inclusive organization of men for the attainment of common ends, the problem of the city should be approached from its political and legal sides. If this outline of problems shall serve to suggest to the student the possibilities of the study of city government and of the general city problem, and shall be of any value to him as a guide in his further work, the publication of this volume will have been worth while.

My acknowledgments are especially due to the

great work already done in the study of municipal problems by Dr. Albert Shaw and Professor Frank J. Goodnow. I am under particular obligations to Professor Goodnow for instruction and advice during my connection with Columbia University as a student of administration, and for his kindness in reading the manuscript of this work and making suggestions and corrections. My thanks are also due to a large number of city officials who have furnished me with municipal documents.

DELOS F. WILCOX.

RAISINVILLE, MICH.,
6th August, 1897.

TABLE OF CONTENTS

CHAPTER I

INTRODUCTORY 1

 The unit of political interest — Importance of local institutions — The modern city — The new problems brought by it — The city destroys uniform local government — Unity of government necessary within the city — The city is more than a locality — Area of cities — The study of the city as such — The temporary enthusiasm of reform — The legal position of the city — Purpose of the present work — Divisions of the study.

CHAPTER II

THE PROBLEMS OF FUNCTION 14

 Politics deals with actual functions of government — Analysis of functions — External and internal functions — Religion — Foreign relations — The reception of distinguished visitors — Nature of internal functions — Business and politics in city government — Evils of the spoils system — Distinction between primary and secondary functions — Secondary functions are generally less political — Business methods and the raising of revenue — Primary functions — The maintenance of public safety by physical force — Military organization — Execution of warrants and judicial decisions — Protection against fire and flood — Protection of public health — Contagious diseases — Removal of refuse — Removal of the dead — Provision of proper housing — Provision of light, air, and means for recreation — The city's food supply — Administration of justice — Prosecution of criminals — Protection of personal and property rights — Enforcement of police ordinances — Care of defectives and dependents — Relief of the poor — The insane and the idiotic — Physical defectives — Orphan and outcast children — Protective and socialistic functions distinguished — Promotion of economic activity and thrift — Coinage — Banks and pawnshops — Industrial protection — Distribution of information — Furnishing of opportunities for self-help — Levelling up of industrial depressions — Creation of private corporations — Preservation of natural resources — Execution of internal improvements — Rendering of common public services — Transportation facilities furnished — Maintenance of terminals — Public institutions for common service — Distribution of water, light, and heat — Supply of water and electric power — Idealistic functions — Public education — General, professional, and technical schools — Public libraries — Museums, gardens, art galleries, etc. — Musical and theatrical exhibitions — Promotion of public morality — Suppression of vice — Maintenance of reformatory institutions — Establishment of a code of law — Secondary functions — Difficulty of classification — Raising revenue for the support of government — The burdens and the benefits of government — Sources of private income and of public revenue compared — Governmental property — Loans — Gifts and legacies — General and special taxation — General police regulation — Public works — City offices and buildings — Municipal gasworks, waterworks, etc. — Public inspection — Gathering statistics — Inspection of food and drink products — Inspection of buildings — Inspection of semi-public institutions — Governmental self-inspection — Provision for the expression of the public will — Elections — Referendum — Hearings, petitions, and popular initiative — Corporate representation — Before the general legislature — Before the general administrative authorities — In relations with coördinate corporations — In the courts — Distribution of functions between central and local governments — Growth of central control — Its necessity.

CHAPTER III

THE PROBLEMS OF CONTROL 72

Sources of control — Control by the people directly — Control by the central government — Relation of the city to the state — The city-state — Absolute independence — Dependent alliance — The feudal city — Mediæval cities in Italy — In England — The commonwealth city — The city in constitutional law — In national constitutions — In commonwealth constitutions — Guarantee of local self-government — Local choice of local officers — In New York, Michigan, and other states — Local charter-framing — In Missouri, California, and Washington — City conventions in New York — The Minnesota plan — Prohibition of special legislation — Local veto in New York — Limitation of municipal financial powers — Municipal debt and popular control — Maximum tax rates — Provisions for particular cities — The city as a creature and agent of the government — Sphere of central control — Local administration in the Hawaiian Republic — Central control over municipal areas — Over police administration — Over public health — Over judicial administration — Over public charity — Over public education — Over local finance — Methods of central control — Legislative control — Judicial control — Administrative control — Appointment and removal of officers — Issuance of instructions — Approval of local by-laws and projects — Hearing of appeals from local decisions — Grant of financial aid — Central control in New South Wales and Victoria — Administrative control in the United States.

CHAPTER IV

THE PROBLEMS OF ORGANIZATION 115

Local importance of organization — General interest in the forms of city government — Analysis of the problems of organization — The municipal electorate — The qualification of citizenship — Great importance of citizenship in American cities — Residence qualifications — Age — Sex — Economic condition — Tax-paying — Class systems in Prussia and Austria — In Australia — Family condition — Educational qualifications — Membership in extra-governmental organizations — Municipal freedom — Disqualifications for the suffrage — Civil divisions of cities — Electoral districts — In Liverpool — In New York — In Paris and London — Administrative districts — In Paris, Vienna, London, and New York — Principles governing the division of a city into districts — Equal representation — Convenience of administration — Necessity of fostering local unity — Divisions of Greater New York — The municipal council — Its position in England — In Germany — In France — In the United States — Qualifications of members — Election areas — General and local representation — Minority representation — The Bridgeport scheme — Proportional representation — Class representation — Methods of nomination — By nominating conventions — By petition — In England — In Australia and Canada — Term of service — Size of councils — Size of American commonwealth legislatures — Organization of council into chambers — The bicameral and the unicameral systems in American cities — Methods of procedure — Special majorities in the Greater New York charter — Committees of the council — Sessions of the council — Powers of the council — Over its own organization — General legislative powers — Enumeration of powers and general grants — The power of taxation — Corporate powers — Powers of direct administration — Judicial powers — Control over municipal officers — Duties of the council — Limitations of the council — Emoluments of councilmen — Salaries and compulsory service — Head of the corporation — Importance of the mayor in American cities — In French, German, and English cities — How the mayor is chosen — Election by the people — Election by the council — Appointment by the central government — Term of service

— Official position — Legislative powers — The veto power in American and German cities — Mayor's indirect legislative powers in Greater New York — Judicial powers of the mayor — Administrative powers — The mayor and the police department — Privileges of the mayoralty — In England — In France — The mayor's salary — Separation of executive and administrative functions — The administrative departments — Their number and spheres of activity — In Brooklyn — In Greater New York — In Boston — In other cities — Relations of the departments to each other — The cabinet system — The administrative system tried in New Orleans — Heads of departments — Election by the council — By the legislature — Appointment by the governor — By the mayor subject to the council's approval — Election by the people — Term of service — Boards and single commissioners — Deliberation and executive efficiency — Bi-partisan boards — The subordinate departmental service — Civil service reform — Recent setbacks in Chicago and New York — Legislative powers of the departments — Special and general ordinances — Importance of the study of individual departments — Employees and commissioner in the New York street cleaning department — The tribute of the sciences to municipal government — The city judiciary — Nationalization of judicial functions — Corporation courts — Police courts most important at present time — Local courts of the general system — New York's experience — Appointment and tenure of judge — Judicial procedure — Ministerial officers of the judiciary — Public prosecution — The jury system — How it is affected by city conditions — Centralization of responsibility — Rascality and incapacity in official service — The egotism of democracy — Centralization of responsibility is a makeshift — Organization is the fixing of responsibility — No uniform system is possible — The dictatorial mayoralty is not likely to be permanent.

CHAPTER V

CONCLUDING REMARKS 234

The city is a part of the general administrative system — Reasons for isolating the city for study — The city is the door to socialism — Vast municipal expenditures — Effect of city life on the political capacity of citizens — Haste and superficial culture — Social disintegration in cities — Destruction of neighborhood and family life — The ebb and flow of civilization — Expansion of municipal functions — Concluding summary of political problems — Government must be made interesting to the citizens — Democracy is at stake.

LIST OF AUTHORITIES 245

GENERAL INDEX 249

THE STUDY OF CITY GOVERNMENT

CHAPTER I

INTRODUCTORY

§ 1. The unit of political interest. — The unit of political science during the prime of ancient civilization was the city-state. The city with its outlying territory was the unit of commerce, of civilization, of war, and of law and political organization.[1] Under Roman influence the political unit came to be the military empire, dominated by the capital city at first, and then by the imperial legions. Local institutions were neglected and Europe plunged into the Dark Ages. It was the development of new vigor in the political life of the localities that heralded the dawn of modern times. In the later middle ages cities grew up as centres of trade and commerce in Italy, France, Germany, England, and Spain. It was the rise

---

[1] The little book by Professor W. W. Fowler, entitled *The City State of the Greeks and Romans*, gives a fascinating and scholarly account of the political organization and ideals of the ancient city. The origin, rise, and decadence of the city as the unit of political organization in Greece and Italy are carefully portrayed.

of the towns that struck the deathblow to feudalism. Wealth and intelligence centred in the cities, and the special needs of the urban populations gave rise to new forms of political organization. The spirit of freedom was developed, and a persistent struggle for local self-government was carried on for centuries.[1] Through the help of the sturdy burghers the kings were enabled to build up modern national states. And afterwards it was the burghers also who led in the struggle for wider political representation, and brought about the nationalization of municipal freedom.[2] Thus in modern times again the unit has been enlarged and political interest has centred in the larger state. This inevitable and irrepressible expansion of the sphere of political relations is always a subject of absorbing interest. Even now our passion for universality leads us to predict the coming of the world-state presently.[3] There is danger that unless we rein in our enthusiasm one of those repetitions for which history is justly famed will require us to begin all over again and build up rational

---

[1] For an account of the English towns and their struggles for freedom, see Mrs. J. R. Green's two-volume work, *Town Life in the Fifteenth Century.*

[2] See Dareste de la Chavanne, *Histoire de l'Administration en France*, Vol. I., pp. 174–219.

[3] See a paper by Professor J. W. Burgess on "Political Science and History," read before the American Historical Society, December, 1896, and published in the *American Historical Review*, April, 1897.

political institutions from the bottom. While our attention has been fixed upon the national state, the theory and practice of local government have been partially neglected. Hon. Nathan Matthews has eloquently said:[1] "The great questions of state and national politics make more interesting subjects for popular discussion than the dry details of municipal administration; but, after all, the questions that will touch you oftenest and closest in your personal relations are questions of municipal rather than of state or national government. . . . We are working out a problem that has received no attention from the educated intelligence of mankind since the days of classic Greece — the problem of self-government on democratic principles for great bodies of people congregated together in a single neighborhood, and without the controlling power of a superior central government." In the United States the national government has nothing to do with city administration save in the single city of Washington. And although the state legislatures constitute a "controlling power of a superior central government," this control is very different from that exercised over cities in other parts of the world and in former ages.

[1] *The City Government of Boston*, note, pp. 182–185. Mr. Matthews was mayor of Boston during the four years, 1891–95, and this book is his farewell address to the council with accompanying documents. It is a valuable contribution to the discussion of municipal problems.

§ 2. The modern city. — While the relation of the city to the state has been going through this course of development, there have come changes in the conditions of local government itself which cannot be overlooked. Chief among them is the advent of the modern city with its feverish activity and its resistless force. The student of politics is at a loss to know just how this disturbing element should be disposed of. We hear constantly of the cities as places where population is congested, as though city life itself were a disease, as though men, like hills of corn, must needs be planted a certain number of feet apart in order to live and grow normally.[1] There is a certain mental fascination in the conditions of urban life that seems to be in many ways like the power which alcoholic and narcotic stimulants exercise over the physical organism. At any rate the term "congestion" is properly applied to the conditions of life in the most crowded districts of large cities. And in so far as the congestion of population is due to the

---

[1] The general outcry against the evils of city life is so well known that specific references are hardly necessary here. It may be well, however, to quote from a source not very familiar to the general public. In commenting upon the evils of unjust discrimination between different cities and towns in the matter of railroad rates, by which the concentration of population at a few points has been stimulated, the Interstate Commerce Commission, in its *Second Annual Report*, 1888, p. 32, made use of the following language: "It will probably not be claimed by any one that it is desirable to give by law, or through the use of public conveniences, an artificial stimulus

artificial stimulus offered by the misdirected development of the transportation system or to other preventable causes, we have on our hands, doubtless, a genuine social disease. This disease must, however, be treated intelligently by the public and by the state, and must be carefully distinguished from the apparently normal tendency of people to gather into cities for nearly every pursuit except agriculture. Many have tried to shame the city out of its existence by cursing its vices or lamenting over its allurements. This method of dealing with the city problem has signally failed. The city is steadily absorbing the wealth and the population of the world.[1] If city life be indeed a disease, the plague of plagues has reached us. None but inveterate pessimists can accept this conclusion. In the very conditions of city life we must find or make some contribution to the ends of rational

to the building up of cities at the expense of the country. In great cities great social and political evils always concentrate, grow, and strengthen, and the larger the cities are the more difficult it is to bring these evils under legal or moral restraints. This fact is so generally recognized that the feeling may be said to be practically universal that the interest of any country is best consulted when public measures and the employment of public conveniences favor the diffusion of population and the profitable employment of industrial energy everywhere, rather than the concentration of population in few localities."

[1] For statistics of urban and rural wealth and population in the United States, see an article by Mr. C. F. Emerick, entitled "An Analysis of Agricultural Discontent in the United States," *Political Science Quarterly*, Vol. XI., pp. 435-449 (September, 1896).

evolution.[1] At any rate the city is here and must be governed. And it cannot be governed in the old way as an independent or semi-independent political unit. It must keep its place as a subordinate part of the all-absorbing state. This fact has introduced an immediate and important complication into the problem of local government. Great aggregations of people must be governed as subordinate units within the national state. And yet they must be self-governing, and as far as possible free from the interference of the central authorities. Such is the problem of government presented by the modern city under the prevailing system of democratic institutions. The civic spirit that existed in the ancient cities as a result of their political independence is a force which cannot be counted on at the present day.

§ 3. **The city fatal to uniform local government.**—The modern city offers an essentially new problem of government from another standpoint also. The mere existence of a city confounds the easy uniformity of local government. The lines of county, township, school district, parish, are blotted out by the essential conditions

[1] See Dr. Albert Shaw's well-known book, *Municipal Government in Great Britain*, pp. 1-19. Dr. Shaw says, p. 2: "Since life in cities, under new and artificial conditions, is henceforth the providential lot assigned to the majority of families, it is to be accepted as a permanent fact for this generation and its immediate successors; and the inevitable order is not to be rebelled against as an evil, but welcomed as if it were the most desirable of destinies."

of city life. This fact becomes evident when we think of the necessary unity in the administration of any particular governmental function in a city. It would be ludicrous to separate the people of the city into local sections for the autonomous performance of public functions, such as building streets, providing a water supply, protecting property from fire, maintaining peace, preserving public health, etc. In spite of the necessary unity in the authority of local government in cities, we shall see later on that a permanent division into districts is desirable in order to develop local interest and keep the people directly in touch with the administration. But the survival of old local divisions within a great city, unless the functions of government are transferred to the central authority or put under its supervision and control, causes great confusion and waste. The example of London, which till recently was governed by a bewildering multitude of local authorities, is instructive here.[1] Chicago furnishes perhaps the best example of any American city where localism has brought confusion and inefficiency. There are separate townships and park districts and a sanitary district partly or wholly within the city limits. The assessment of property for taxation is done by local assessors elected annually in the towns; and this function has become little more than a farce

[1] See Sydney Webb, *The London Programme*, Chaps. II. and III.

and a fraud.¹ It is clear that the government of cities cannot be uniform with township and county government. The old problems of local government are so intensified in cities that they become essentially new problems.² Locality itself is almost destroyed. Who would think of Paris, the heart of the world's culture, with its two and a half millions of people, as a locality? And yet its territorial extent of thirty square miles is less than the area of one of the regular six-miles-square townships of our Central and Western States. Berlin has an area of 24.3 square miles; Glasgow, of 18.5; London (county), of 117.9; Chicago, of 187.1; Philadelphia, of 129.4; Boston, of 43.1; New York (1897), of 62.4; Greater New York (1898), of 317. In 1893 the tenth ward of New York, with an area of 106 acres or about one-sixth of a square mile, had a population of 66,383.³

---

[1] See an article by Robert H. Whitten, entitled "The Assessment of Taxes in Chicago," *Journal of Political Economy*, Vol. V., p. 175 (March, 1897).

[2] See Prof. F. J. Goodnow, *Municipal Problems*, pp. 183 *et seq.* The increased importance of highways in cities, for example, is well brought out in these words: "The rural highway becomes the city street, which must not only sustain an immense amount of surface traffic to which the rural highway is not subjected, but must serve as a means of conveying under its surface water, gas, heat, electricity, and sewerage. Often, in the case of large cities, the street is made use of as a means of carrying passengers and merchandise beneath its surface."

[3] See *Report of Tenement House Committee of 1894*, New York, p. 257.

At that rate an area of thirty-six square miles, or the equivalent of an ordinary Western township, would have a population of more than fourteen millions. Although limited area is the fundamental fact in "locality," yet a vast population will destroy many of the characteristics of locality, in spite of a small area. Political institutions are based upon population as well as upon territory. The more complex forms of social and political organization are to a great extent independent of territorial areas. All the conditions that made a uniform system of local self-government possible are swept away by the rise of cities. Without cities government could to a large extent partake of the simplicity of a machine. With cities it must have the complexity of an organism.

§ 4. **The study of the city as such.** — As a result of necessity, learned in the school of sad experience, we have turned our attention fitfully from the exciting problems of national politics to local government in cities. It is a common source of regret to reformers that the interest of the people in municipal government is fitful. With a great show of indignation and enthusiasm a citizens' or reform ticket is elected in isolated cities at long intervals of time, when some great revelation of municipal corruption has been made. Then the people settle back into their ordinary condition of apathy, and the spoilsmen work their way back into power by shrewdly and persistently calling attention to the mistakes, big and little, which an inexperienced reform government inevitably makes. As a result of the intermittent attention paid to the problems of the city, no satisfactory and persistent theory of municipal institutions has been developed, at least in the United States. It would indeed be somewhat illogical to study city government as such and attempt to formulate a peculiar theory of its form and functions. Government, like the state, must be ultimately a unit. All of its grades and departments must be coordinated and correlated so that the unity of the state's purpose shall be fulfilled. But as a matter of fact, hardly any one as yet seems to have discovered the exact relations of the city in the general scheme of political organization. Professor Goodnow has made the most notable contributions to the solution of this generally neglected problem.[1] The city has looked so much like a pathological phenomenon, and it has so upset the simplicity of the machinery of government, that students and legislators alike have been in most cases a good deal bewildered. To get a clear view is the pressing problem. For this purpose it is perhaps

---

[1] Professor Goodnow has published three books which treat of municipal relations: *Comparative Administrative Law*, 2 vols., 1893; *Municipal Home Rule*, 1895; and *Municipal Problems*, 1897. The last of these books marks a great advance in the scientific discussion of the problem of city government in the United States, by presenting a pretty definite programme of reform, based upon careful thought and wide study of municipal systems.

allowable to study city government in a considerable degree of isolation. According to Professor Goodnow's view, possibly, it would seem unwise to isolate the city at all for purposes of study. He would have us take the city as it is, primarily an agent of the state government in our American polity at least, and study municipal government simply as a part of a general system of administration. From the legal standpoint this method is undoubtedly the best for an American student. But it is nevertheless true that the city is a *social* fact, and on its social side it is largely independent of any particular national system of public law. It is also true that, historically, cities were first chartered primarily as industrial corporations, and that they still retain to some extent their private corporate functions. It is the purpose of the present writer to present an outline of the problems of city government which will include more than the merely public law problems of the American city. The effort will be made to make a general analysis applicable to the study of government in any of its grades or branches, and to fill in the outline more in detail for the special study of city problems. The same general scheme may easily be filled in and carried out into detail by any student more especially concerned with the problems of national or commonwealth government. By formulating a plan of study applicable to all government, and applying it to the special field of the city, we may hope to get on towards symmetry in our political theories.

§ 5. **Divisions of the study.** — In every act of organized bodies three preliminary steps are taken. First, of course, comes the formulation of the project itself, the determination of *what* is to be done. Then follows the choice of a manager to take charge of the enterprise. And lastly the working force is organized. Translated into political terms, this process is nothing else than the solution of the problems of governmental functions, governmental control, and governmental organization. As applied to municipalities the process is the determination of what the city shall do for its citizens, of how it shall be controlled, whether by the people or by the central authorities of the state, and of how the municipal machinery shall be organized. In treating of city government specially, we have to consider not only the general question of what are governmental functions, but also the question of the distribution of these functions between local and central authorities. It is to be recognized that *every* classification of problems in the more complex sciences must be inexact. One set of problems reacts upon another. For instance, the distribution of functions between local and central governments may depend largely upon the governmental organization and the methods and extent of the central control over the local authorities. All analysis must be followed by synthesis. It would be idle to isolate any object for purposes of study, if we were to *leave* it in isolation. The city is no exception. It is the purpose of this writing to present in a tentative form an outline of the problems of function, the problems of control, and the problems of organization of city government.

CHAPTER II

THE PROBLEMS OF FUNCTION

§ 6. Governmental functions. — To the politician, whether practical or theoretical, all the functions that the government actually undertakes are governmental functions. What these functions shall be is determined by the caprice or the judgment of the sovereign body. If that body is intelligent, it is guided by the advice of the economist, the sociologist, and the politician. But the politician's advice is only negative, and often little heeded. He plays the eminently conservative rôle of quoting from his experience to show what cannot be done by government. It often happens that the citizens of a state, ignorant of the experiences of the past and possessing an unlimited faith in the efficacy of governmental dicta, are anxious to force upon the government functions which from their very nature are impossible of fulfilment by political organs. Laws arbitrarily fixing the prices of mercantile products, interfering with freedom of thought, or attempting to regulate the details of individual action, have been tried and found wanting many times in the world's history. It is the business of the politician or political scientist to learn the lessons of past failures, and to protest against thrusting upon the government any additional function which historical precedents clearly indicate to be impracticable. On the other hand, the economist and the sociologist have a more positive share in the determination of the sphere of governmental activity. It is the task of the economist to distribute between political authorities and private voluntary agencies those functions whose primary purpose is the satisfaction of individual human wants. The sociologist distributes in like manner the functions for the satisfaction of social wants. In other words, the practical task of political economy and sociology is the assignment of functions to the state and its agents on the one hand, and to individuals and voluntary organizations on the other. Politics or political science treats of the methods of fulfilling the functions assigned to the state and its agents. To attempt, therefore, an analysis of the *proper* functions of government, is not the task of political science. Any effort to make a rigid or an exhaustive classification of the *actual* functions of government would be futile. The most useful classification in the study of politics is one that arranges these functions, whether undertaken in one country or in another, in the present or in a past age, around certain groups of purposes as conveniently as possible for the illumination of the problems of control and the problems of organization, which together make up the real task of political science.

§ 7. **External functions: religion.** — Perhaps the most obvious classification of functions is into external and internal. The principles of action are quite different where the government is dealing with powers outside of itself, and where it is dealing with its citizens or with parts of its own framework, such as cities, townships, departments, etc. The external functions of government may be divided into two classes, — those in which the government acts in relation to a supernatural power, God; and those in which the government deals with other governments. Here we have religious worship and foreign affairs as functions of government. In ancient times cities were extremely religious.[1] Public worship was the most important function of the governmental authorities. Every student of the history of ancient Greece and Rome is more or less familiar with the religious activities of the archons, consuls, and priests. Religious festivals, processions, celebrations, sacrifices, etc., were constantly engaged in by the political authorities. In mediæval Venice, also, when a new Doge was to be chosen, one of the privy councillors repaired to the cathedral and petitioned the Deity for his

---

[1] See Fustel de Coulanges, *The Ancient City*, Chaps. VI. and VII.; and Fowler, *op. cit.*, pp. 33, 45, 69.

blessing on the election.[1] Even to-day in Germany and parts of Switzerland the municipal authorities have certain functions to perform in connection with the churches.[2] But these functions are administrative rather than directly religious. Religion has so far ceased to be a function of city government that we may regard it as important from the historical standpoint only.

§ 8. **Foreign affairs.** — It may, perhaps, seem hardly logical to speak of foreign affairs as a "function" of government. By the term "foreign affairs" is meant the task of every independent state in maintaining its identity and integrity in the family of states. Foreign affairs include all those activities of government by which it represents its subjects as a sovereign unit in relation to other sovereign units. Since the entrance of the free cities, Hamburg, Bremen, and Lübeck, into the German Empire, there is no important example left of cities which attend to foreign affairs.[3] Ancient and mediæval cities

---

[1] Henry Mann, *Ancient and Mediæval Republics*, p. 522.

[2] Goodnow, *Comparative Administrative Law*, Vol. I., p. 318; H. de Ferron, *Institutions Municipales et Provinciales Comparées*, p. 225. In the latest accounts of the city of Dundee, Scotland, published for the year ending July 31, 1896, we find a statement of receipts of the five "city churches."

[3] The North German Union was founded in 1867, while the present German Empire came into existence on January 1st, 1871. The free cities were members of the former as of the latter. See Burgess, *Political Science and Constitutional Law*, Vol. I., pp. 114 *et seq.*

were constantly engaged in making war or carrying on negotiations with other cities and states. About the only vestige of this condition of things is to be found in the receptions sometimes given to distinguished foreign visitors by the mayors of great cities. In his recent visit to the United States, Li Hung Chang was publicly received by the mayors of New York and Philadelphia. He was also received in Scotland by the corporation of Glasgow.[1] On the occasion of the presentation of the Grant monument to New York city, April 27, 1897, the mayor gave the hospitality of the city to many distinguished guests. The reception of great personages seems to be more important in the British cities than in American towns. In Great Britain the Lords Mayor and the Lords Provost, as heads of the municipal corporations, have important ceremonial and functionary duties to perform. Formerly the Lord Mayor of London received foreign visitors with great pomp and *éclat*. Only a year or two ago, Hon. Thomas F. Bayard, United States ambassador to the court of St. James, was granted the freedom of the city by the corporation of Dundee.[2] It is true that sometimes the foreign relations of a European

---

[1] See the Lord Provost's *Résumé of New Work*, for the year 1895–96.

[2] In the *Corporation Accounts* of Dundee for the year 1895–96 we find this item : " Extraordinary casual expenditure — Outlays in connection with Freedom of City to Hon. T. F. Bayard, £42 16s."

state are appreciably affected by the attitude of the people of the capital city; but so far as the legal position of the city is concerned, we may practically ignore foreign affairs as a function of modern municipalities. External functions, and especially foreign affairs, cease to be attended to by the city as soon as that unit is fully subordinated to the wider state. In this outline, therefore, we may confine ourselves chiefly to a classification of internal functions. Here, at least, the duties of the city are not wholly obsolete.

§ 9. **Business and politics in city government.**[1] — Before taking up the classification of the internal functions of the city, we should consider for a moment the real nature of these functions as a whole. Some years ago, and, indeed, until very recently, municipal reformers generally raised the cry of "business, not politics" in reference to city government. There seems to be at the present time a healthful reaction, born of wider knowledge and saner judgment, toward the recognition of the essentially political character of cities. Professor Goodnow has shown conclusively that we cannot hope for the permanent exclusion of party contests from municipal elections as long as we have state and national party government.[2] The functions of

[1] For a discussion of the position of the city as regards politics and business, see Goodnow, *Municipal Problems*, especially Chap. II. and pp. 57 and 185.

[2] *Ibid.*, Chap. VIII., "Municipal Government and National Political Parties."

a city, where all male residents are eligible to the right of suffrage, must certainly be political in the broad sense of that term. The man who claims that the city is a business corporation, and should be conducted primarily on business, as opposed to political, principles, ought to admit frankly his close kinship to the socialist. For if the whole people residing within a given district, and possessing governmental power, are thereby constituted a business corporation, what more can socialism claim? The fact is, that with the extension of the suffrage, cities have become less and less business corporations, and have become more and more political agents, until at the present time it is hardly worth while to distinguish between the business functions of city government and those of national government. Professor Goodnow says the city is "primarily an organ for local government — for the satisfaction of local needs," and "secondarily an agent of state government."[1] If this distinction be a true one, we must remember that even in the former of these capacities the city is not a business corporation but an agent of the people in their sovereign capacity, and in so far is coördinate with the central state government itself. In other words, as has been so often contended by the courts of Michigan, the city has a place in our fundamental law back of written constitutions.[2] The real impor-

[1] *Municipal Problems*, p. 26.
[2] See *People* vs. *Hurlbut*, 24 Mich. 44. For citation of other

tance of the outcry against politics in city government lies in the prevalence of the spoils system in all the grades of government in the United States. The spoils system has been at its worst in cities because the issues of national politics have dominated local politics, — largely for sentimental reasons, — and because in the cities there have been vast expenditures of money. It is to the handling of public funds that the spoils system devotes itself. *There are to be found its sinews of war.* The real significance of the distinction between business and politics in all governmental administration, including that of cities, will be shown more clearly by the classification of functions.

§ **10. Primary and secondary functions.** — It is evident that the immediate purpose of raising revenue differs radically from the purpose of public instruction, public lighting, or poor relief. Raising revenue is not undertaken for its own sake, but simply as a necessary method of getting means for the fulfilment of the primary functions, all of which are comprised in the promotion of the public welfare. City halls and schoolhouses are not built simply for the sake of building them, but for use

---

cases, see Wilcox, *Municipal Government in Michigan and Ohio*, Chap. III. The case of *Crawfordsville* vs. *Braden*, 130 Indiana, 149, should also be consulted. The doctrine of the Michigan courts has even found its way into New York. In a very recent case, *Rathbone* vs. *Wirth*, 150 N. Y. 459, the dicta of the judges lean very strongly toward the Michigan view of local self-government.

in the performance of direct functions. Tenement houses are inspected and censuses taken, not for the mere sake of doing these things, but in order to further the public ends. Elections are held, not for their own sake, but to get an expression of the public will. These illustrations go to show that the functions of government may be roughly classed as direct and indirect, or primary and secondary. Of course, all of these functions ultimately centre in one purpose, the fulfilment of the will of the state, which is the public wellbeing. This classification, although of necessity imperfect and inexact, will throw some light upon the question of the relations of business and politics, which was discussed in the preceding section. The primary functions of government, whose direct and immediate purpose is to promote the general welfare, are all political. The secondary functions, whose direct purpose is to furnish means for the fulfilment of the primary functions, are immediately political only as they affect the personal or property rights of the citizens. To illustrate by analogy, we see the city contracting with some individual for the execution of a public work. The contractor is bound by certain specifications and restricted by certain limitations. The work must be of a quality described, and must be done within a given time. In the performance of the work the contractor must not infringe upon certain rights of private individuals, and perhaps he is even required to pay his workmen a certain wage, or at certain fixed intervals. But after all the obligations of the contractor have been considered, we always find some room left for discretion. Here the contractor works for his own private interest, and the city is not concerned. Nearly the same is true of government. In the performance of its secondary functions, within certain limitations imposed upon it by the public will and the public welfare, the government acts for its own private interest. The people are concerned that the primary functions of government be performed, and that their own personal and property rights be not infringed beyond a certain point. These conditions fulfilled, the people have no immediate interest whether the government expends much effort or little. In a republic, of course, where the government is taken by rotation from the ranks of the people, all who are eligible to office become individually and collectively interested in even the private welfare of the government. In proportion as government becomes more democratic and more immediately responsive to the popular will, these semi-private interests of the governing organization are done away with, and the last vestige of business motives disappears from the conduct of public affairs. But with these limitations in view, and under the present imperfectly democratic *régime*, we may say that business methods and business motives are largely applicable to the secondary functions of government. The raising of revenue furnishes the most noteworthy illustration of this proposition and its limitations. If the city gets its revenue from property owned and managed as a lucrative investment, the government has almost complete liberty in the adoption of business methods. But if revenue is raised by taxation, where the property rights of the citizens are directly concerned, the government must adapt itself to public prejudices and get money from the least obnoxious kind of tax, though the tax itself may be a wretched and expensive means from the standpoint of the government's private or business interests. The science of politics is above all a science of method, of ways and means, and the further we get on the road from the question *what* to the question *how* in matters of governmental function, the more intense and pertinent political interest becomes.

I. *Primary Functions*

§ 11. The maintenance of public safety by physical force. — The fundamental basis of all government is the organization of the aggregate physical force of the whole body of citizens for the protection of well-disposed individuals from the lawless attacks of the anti-social classes, and from the destructive forces of nature, and for the protection of tribe, state, or nation as a whole from the onslaughts of hostile political units. The whole idea of sovereignty is based upon *might*, and the ultimate resource of government is always physical power. The use of physical force in the maintenance of public safety may take three principal directions.

(*a*) Invasions, insurrections, riots, and disorders are prevented or suppressed by the organization of force. In cities the police officers perform this among other functions. The organization of the militia in the United States is by localities, and though the county is usually the unit for this purpose, there are examples where city and county government are practically merged. The active military organization has become pretty thoroughly nationalized in modern times, but in the past this organization has been provided by the city, of course, in so far as the city has been identical with the state. The feudal cities, as well as the ancient city-states, often had their own armies, and were not slow to use them against each other. The soldiers of the city of London played an important rôle in the early internal and other wars of England.[1] Even to-day Dr. Lewis G. Janes speaks of the "quasi-militant structure of the European city."[2] Indeed, during the great Civil War many

---

[1] See Firth, *Municipal London*, Chap. I.; Loftie, *Historic Towns —London*, Chap. IX.; and Norton, *The City of London*, p. 56.

[2] *The Problem of City Government*, a lecture delivered before the Brooklyn Ethical Association, and published as No. 6 in *Man and*

American cities of the Northern States gave bounties to soldiers. The city and county of New York spent many millions of dollars for this purpose.[1] Boston also adopted this policy.[2] A large amount of money has been expended, and is still being expended, by the city of New York for the construction and maintenance of armories.

(b) A second channel for the use of organized force by the government is through the execution of warrants and judicial decisions. This function is carried out in municipalities by police officers, constables, marshals, sheriffs, prison wardens, and similar officers. Under the preceding head were classed the necessary uses of physical force by the political organization of society against the attacks of masses of people or social units. In the present case we treat of the use of physical force as directed against refractory individuals, generally criminals or disorderly persons. This function of government also is a good deal centralized. The management of prisons, especially, is in most countries made a part of the central administration. But the maintenance of the peace is still regarded as a local function in many of the American commonwealths, in accordance with the historic

---

the State, and as a separate pamphlet, *Evolution Series*, No. 23, February 1, 1892, D. Appleton and Co., New York. See p. 156.

[1] See Dr. E. Dana Durand, *The Finances of New York City*, soon to be published in book form.

[2] Matthews, *op. cit.*, p. 51.

doctrine of local self-government. In Michigan the Supreme Court has held that constables are local peace officers provided for by the constitution, and cannot be superseded by a metropolitan police force under state control.[1]

(c) A third direction in which physical force is commonly employed by government, is for the defence of the people against disasters caused by the natural elements, such as fire, wind, and flood. The fire departments of cities attend to the prevention, extinguishment, and investigation of conflagrations. There are sometimes, also, local commissions to look after levees and dykes. The ocean dykes of Holland and the levees along the Mississippi River are examples of works maintained by government for the defence of life and property against flood. The Mississippi levees, at least, are maintained in part by local and in part by state authorities. Government has not yet effected much in the way of resisting the cyclone and the hurricane. But the work of the United States Weather Bureau may be regarded in a sense as intended to prepare the people for defence against storms. Such disasters as the St. Louis cyclone of 1896 may lead cities themselves to take steps for the protection of their people and their property against the ravages of the wind.

---

[1] See *Allor* vs. *Wayne County Auditors*, 43 Mich. 76. See also *People* vs. *Albertson*, 55 N. Y. 50.

§ 12. **The protection of public health.** — The protection of the health of the community by governmental agencies may be regarded as a form of protection by physical force against the ravages of disease. The forces to be vanquished are, however, generally much more subtle than armies, mobs, murderers, conflagrations, and floods. In undertaking the protection of the public health, the government does not attempt to guarantee the health of the individual citizen against the effects of his own carelessness or profligacy. The government interferes only when the people are put in danger of disease and death through each other's negligence, or through the conditions of life over which individuals have little or no control. The crowding of population into cities, it may easily be seen, is the result of great social and industrial forces, and tends to enlarge very greatly the interference of government for the protection of the public health. The lives of thousands may be endangered by one man's negligence. Health is protected or promoted in a variety of ways, and a very large share of the activities of government in a great city minister directly or indirectly to the accomplishment of this end.

(*a*) First, of course, there is the direct prevention or suppression of disease. In this field municipal boards of health are very active. Unhealthy food and drink products are destroyed, the sick are segregated in hospitals, medical care is given them, medical inspection is provided for the children in the public schools, clothes and houses are disinfected, and nuisances are removed. Perhaps Berlin has as perfect a system of health administration as any city in the world. German cities generally have made great progress in sanitary administration.[1] The same may be said of many British and French cities.[2] And, indeed, American cities are beginning to wake up to the importance of the direct protection of public health. The health board of New York city has in recent years taken advanced ground in its warfare against contagious diseases.

(*b*) Second, government in cities provides or supervises and regulates the disposal of refuse. It needs no argument to show how imperative it is that sewage and other forms of waste in great centres of population be removed by governmental agencies or authority. This is necessary, primarily, for the protection of the people's health; and, secondarily, for keeping the avenues of business, travel, and transportation unobstructed. The successful disposal of a great city's sewage,

---

[1] See Pollard, *A Study in Municipal Government: the Corporation of Berlin;* and Dr. Albert Shaw, *Municipal Government in Continental Europe,* Chaps. VI. and VII.

[2] For municipal sanitary administration in Great Britain, see Dolman, *Municipalities at Work;* and Shaw, *Municipal Government in Great Britain.*

garbage, ashes, street dirt, etc., is one of the leading tasks of the municipal authorities.[1] This work is undertaken by the departments of street cleaning, sewerage, public works, health, etc.

(*c*) In the third place, and closely connected with the preceding means of protecting public health, we have the removal of the dead. Paris has a municipal crematory. Many American cities have municipal cemeteries. Practically all cities impose positive restrictions upon the cemeteries managed by private persons. The removal of dead animals is also subject to municipal regulation.

(*d*) In the fourth place, we may consider the regulation or provision of proper housing for the people as a function undertaken by cities directly in the interest of public health. Provision is made by health officers and building inspectors for light, room, and fresh air in tenements and factories. Cities often condemn unsanitary dwellings, and sometimes construct model houses for the working classes. New York city has, during the past year (1896-97), condemned nearly a hundred "rear tenements" as being unfit for habitation. Municipal tenement houses and lodging houses for the poor have been built by the corporation of Glasgow. Liverpool, Dublin, and other British cities, also, have constructed model tenements.

---

[1] For some of the indirect effects of the way sewage and waste are disposed of upon the vitality of the people, see Dr. Janes, *op. cit.*, pp. 178 *et seq.*

(*e*) In the fifth place, the provision of light, air, room, and means of recreation out of doors is, in great cities, one of the most important and most necessary tasks of the public authorities for the preservation of the physical energy of the people. Here we may class the parks, boulevards, commons, and playgrounds so universally demanded of city authorities. Although the immediate purpose of parks, boulevards, and playgrounds is often officially announced as the furnishing of means for the people's recreation, it is evident that, generally, the ultimate purpose is the protection and promotion of the people's health. In nearly every case, the means of recreation furnished by a city may be regarded as a means for the promotion of health or for the encouragement of education. When the furnishing of pleasure or recreation for its own sake comes to be regarded as a primary function of government, we may well believe that society has begun to suffer from over-civilization and luxury. It is as impossible for a sovereign body as for an individual to become a professional pleasure-seeker without demoralization.

(*f*) Lastly, we may speak of the *approvisionnement* of the city, as the French call it, among the means used by municipal authorities to promote the public health. This function is not generally important in modern cities, except occasionally in time of war. But when cities were important military strongholds, and before the steamship and the railway had brought the great centres of population within easy reach of the world's food supply, the problem of provisioning a great city was a task of first-rate importance for the municipal authorities. In France and Italy, at the present time, the provisioning of the large towns assumes a greatly increased importance on account of the *octroi* system of taxation. A city may regulate its *approvisionment*, with full justification, by a comprehensive system of municipal markets, abattoirs, and food inspection. Berlin has followed out this policy with great success.

§ 13. **The administration of public justice.** — This function of government is of importance just in proportion as the theory of individual rights and obligations has become definite. The administration of justice by government means the recognition of private rights and private duties, and the peaceable adjustment of social conflicts by the authoritative interpretation of the rules of law and custom. In this way the arbitrary domination of brute strength and brute impulse is superseded by the rule of organized justice. The work of the judicial authorities takes in the main three directions.

(*a*) There is, first, the prosecution of criminals. This function is regarded as belonging primarily to central officers, yet sometimes city courts have had the power to punish with death even. In the later middle ages, English boroughs had the authority to put to death thieves taken in the act.[1] Indeed, until the English municipal reform act of 1835 was passed, many boroughs continued to exercise very important criminal jurisdiction.[2]

(*b*) In the second place, the judicial function includes the protection of the personal and property rights of citizens and other residents and sojourners. This purpose is accomplished by the civil courts, which are often organized as a part of the city government. The guarantee of civil liberty is usually one of the chief functions of the modern state through its national government. But new rights may be established by local laws, and even general laws are frequently enforced in the first instance by means of courts locally organized.

(*c*) Finally, of particular importance in cities, is the power, almost universally exercised, to enact and enforce general police ordinances. Social relations in cities are so much more complex than in the rural districts, that the police power of the government has to go into great detail in the regulation

---

[1] See Pollock and Maitland, *History of the English Law*, Vol. I., p. 628.

[2] See *The Laws and Customs, Rights, Liberties, and Privileges of the City of London*, published in 1765, by R. Withy and W. Griffin. On pp. 140–196 there is a description of the organization and jurisdiction of the seventeen courts of the old City of London. For the condition throughout England in the boroughs, see J. R. Somers Vine, *English Municipal Institutions*, pp. 149–185.

of individual conduct. In this way individual rights are protected and the public welfare is guarded. The enforcement of such ordinances is entrusted to police officers, licensing authorities, courts of summary jurisdiction, etc. The summary courts are generally, in large cities, specially organized under police justices, city magistrates, or other judicial authorities, whose particular function is to attend to cases involving the violation of local law.

§ 14. **The care of the defective and dependent classes.** — With the development of the idea of human brotherhood and equality of rights, the duty of government to make provision for the unfortunate members of society, who would otherwise come to a premature death, has been more and more fully recognized. The general spirit of humanity, incident upon the growth of Christian civilization, will not permit the political organs of society to stand idly by while citizens die of sheer want or neglect.[1] The function of government here under discussion is differentiated into several forms.

(*a*) First, we have the granting of relief to the poor. This is one of the most universal problems of local government, and it is most important in cities. Very often paupers, or those temporarily

---

[1] See Professor S. N. Patten, *A Theory of Social Forces*, pp. 138–143, published as a supplement to the ANNALS of the American Academy, January, 1896; also Amos G. Warner, *American Charities*, Chaps. I. and XIV., and pp. 126 *et seq.*

in great distress, are victims of forces over which they have no control. In some cases it may even be that the pauper is created by the wasteful or blundering policy of government itself. War, evidently, may make paupers out of formerly thrifty citizens. A mistaken economic or monetary policy which encourages business depressions or financial panics, may force many people into pauperism. In such cases, certainly, the state or the local authorities can do no less than relieve the paupers created by governmental action. But in any case, sentiment, especially in democratic countries, requires that the state relieve the poor in their necessity.

(*b*) A second class requiring state assistance is composed of those persons who are mentally incapable of self-regulation. These are the insane and the idiotic. In many cases such persons are cared for by friends and relatives. But often, especially in the case of the insane, public safety requires their isolation from ordinary social intercourse. Asylums and hospitals are provided for them by cities and other local divisions, as well as by the central government.

(*c*) The government is also called upon to assist persons who are physically defective. Hence we have in many cases the public maintenance of the blind, the crippled, and the deaf and dumb. Schools and institutions are often provided for these classes by local government.

(*d*) Lastly, and most important under this general heading, we find the support and training of orphans and outcast children by public authorities. Homes, nurseries, asylums, juvenile schools, and other institutions for dependent children are often either maintained directly or subsidized by cities. There is a special reason why the government should take care of dependent children. Adult paupers are, many of them, worthless members of society, who have come to dependence through their own vices or thriftlessness. The defective classes can in no case become fully efficient citizens, and hence the preservation of their lives is dictated rather by sentiment than by economic policy. But with children the case is different. There is always the consideration that they are in no way to blame for their dependence. Furthermore there is a possibility in any case of their developing into useful citizens of the state if they live. And finally, unless properly cared for, dependent children are likely, if they survive at all, to grow up into adult paupers or criminals, and spend their lives preying upon society.

§ 15. **Protective and socialistic functions distinguished.** — In the preceding paragraphs we have grouped what may be termed the necessary or *protective* functions of government. It is absolutely necessary that governmental functions should be greatly expanded in cities, even if limited to the bare protection of safety and health. But with the increase of the protective functions in the directions of general police and sanitary administration, it seems natural for cities to take up other and more socialistic functions. In the paragraphs that follow we shall try to outline the principal activities of government which may be called optional, socialistic, or non-protective in the narrow sense. Many of these functions have passed chiefly into the hands of the general government, and do not need to be considered in a study of the present problems of government by cities.

§ 16. **The promotion of economic activity and thrift.** — It is universally recognized that government must do certain things to facilitate economic exchange, or even the production and distribution of wealth. No political organization of a nation or a community can be utterly indifferent to the economic welfare of the individual citizens. It is upon the thrift of the people that the state must thrive. It is particularly true in cities that government must interfere in many cases to promote thrift. City guilds and municipal corporations were originally designed more as local business co-partnerships than as agents of sovereignty. The lingering idea that in some way a city is primarily a business corporation points to a *fact;* namely, that in cities the complexity of commercial relations and the friction between the economic rights of individuals make it especially necessary for municipal corporations to undertake certain economic functions which may be safely left to individual activity in country districts. We may enumerate some of the economic functions of government, merely mentioning those which have passed entirely into the hands of the central authorities.

(*a*) First, there are the coining and regulation of money, a universal function of government which has now passed everywhere into the field of the national administration.

(*b*) Then there is the maintenance or regulation of banks and pawnshops. Paris and other European cities maintain savings banks and pawnshops for the benefit of the people.[1] But banking or the regulation of banking is usually a function of national or commonwealth government.

(*c*) In the third place, the protection, subsidizing, or exemption of industry may be mentioned. Most important here are national protective tariffs and subsidies, but American cities have sometimes helped in the establishment of manufactures by the gift or loan of money or by exemption from taxation. In the case of *Loan Association* vs. *Topeka*,[2] the United States Supreme Court held that a law authorizing Topeka to issue bonds to aid manufacturing establishments, where the proceeds of the bonds were to be turned over to

---

[1] See Shaw, *Municipal Government in Continental Europe*, pp. 112-118, 202-204, 371-373.

[2] 20 Wallace, 655.

private persons or corporations as a gift, was unconstitutional and void. Whether or not this decision is binding outside of the state of Kansas, is a disputed question among constitutional lawyers. At any rate, although this decision was rendered in 1874, there have been many laws passed during more recent years, in Ohio at least, authorizing municipal corporations to borrow money for the purpose of stimulating local manufactures. The practice of many cities in loaning their credit to assist in the building of railroads, turnpikes, canals, and other such improvements, became so common about the middle of this century, and its results were so disastrous to the cities in most cases, that the majority of the later commonwealth constitutions have forbidden the loan of municipal credit to individuals, associations, or corporations.

(*d*) A fourth method of promoting industrial activity is by the distribution of information through governmental agencies. The city of Paris established a labor exchange a few years ago.[1] In New York city also a labor bureau was started in 1896 under state authority. But information is distributed more extensively through census reports and other reports prepared by the general government. The consular service also helps to advertise business enterprises in foreign countries.

(*e*) Another way in which government promotes thrift is by the furnishing of opportunities for self-

[1] Shaw, *op. cit.*, p. 111.

help. The best practical illustration of this function is, perhaps, the recent policy adopted in such cities as Detroit and Buffalo, where poor families have been given the chance to raise potatoes and other vegetables on unoccupied lands in the city limits.[1] Ex-Mayor Pingree, of Detroit, won a national reputation through his introduction into that city of the "potato-patch" scheme.

(*f*) Sometimes, also, the government of a state or city tries to level up an industrial depression. There has been a strong movement in the cities of the United States, during recent hard times, to hurry necessary public improvements in order to give work to the unemployed, and at the same time take advantage of low prices for the benefit of the public. It is urged in behalf of this policy that a city may well undertake its necessary public works when labor and materials are cheapest, and when the greatest number of men are out of employment. This policy is possible because a city does not have to depend upon profits or the sale of its products to avoid bankruptcy. The government, having the power to take money by means of taxation in so far as its income from property

---

[1] An interesting account of the success of the potato-patch scheme is contained in the Message of Mayor Jewitt, of Buffalo, January, 1897, p. 19; and in the messages of Mayor Pingree, of Detroit, 1895, p. 45; 1896, p. 24; 1897, p. 20, and *Report* in the appendix. It is said that this general scheme of relief did not originate with Mr. Pingree, to whom it is usually credited, but was copied from Berlin and perhaps other foreign cities.

is insufficient, fixes its income according to its proposed expenditures. On the other hand, a private person or corporation, not having the sovereign power of taxation, has to regulate and limit expenditures according to realized or probable income. It is evident that a careful and persistent policy on the part of cities might give a good deal of immediate relief from the distress of industrial depressions. Whether the ultimate effect of such a policy would be wholesome and consistent with the full economic responsibility of the individual which is favored by conservative men, is quite another question. Glasgow has more than once in recent years opened "relief works," but they have approached very closely to the borders of public charity.

(g) Perhaps the most important way in which government promotes the industrial development of a community is by the creation of fictitious persons, or corporations with legal powers and rights. Cities do not participate directly in this function of government, at least in modern times. And yet cities have much to do with the forms, powers, and limitations of corporate bodies organized within the municipal limits. In so far as cities have control of public franchises, the municipal authorities by their positive acts make the existence of street railway companies, ferry companies, gas and electric lighting companies, water companies, etc., possible. The tremendous importance of the mere creation of corporations — legal bodies, each composed of a group of individuals — for the encouragement of trade, industry, and economic enterprise in the great centres of wealth and population, is frequently lost sight of by the student of government.

(*h*) The preservation of natural resources is ordinarily the task of general governmental agencies. Forests, fisheries, and game are frequently protected by the commonwealth or national authorities. Under the early charters of New York city, the royalties of hunting, hawking, fishing, etc., were granted to the corporation.[1] The City of London, by its old charters, was given power to protect the Thames fisheries. The limited area and the vast population of modern cities make the preservation of such natural resources within the municipal limits generally impracticable.

(*i*) Finally, government, both general and local, often undertakes the execution of what are called in the United States "internal improvements." Roads, railroads, canals, and harbors have often been constructed or subsidized by cities. The Manchester Ship Canal and the deepening of the Clyde at Glasgow are notable examples of this policy. The Cincinnati Southern Railroad, constructed and owned by the city of Cincinnati, may fairly be brought under the head of "internal improvements."

---

[1] See Dongan Charter, 1686, section 3; and Montgomerie Charter, 1730, section 37.

§ 17. The rendering of public services, generally of a monopolistic nature. — In cities, by reason of concentration of population, the natural local supply of water becomes inadequate for the needs of the people. Hence it is necessary for some common agent to step in and bring the supply of water from a distance. The conditions of city life further make an artificial supply of light necessary. There are reasons why it is practicable and desirable for a single agency to furnish this supply. The same is true of the various forms of transportation. The city dweller cannot serve himself. His world of activity is too complex. He must depend for most things upon the help of others. Especially he must be rendered certain services by a common agent, which is either the government or some one authorized and regulated by the government. The exhaustion of the local resources of nature, and especially the necessity for economizing space and time, tend irresistibly toward the consolidation of the agencies of service.[1] Let us see specifically some of the common services more or less under the control of government.

(*a*) In the first place, there is transportation. Roads and streets are almost everywhere main-

---

[1] It should be noted that technically municipal monopolies are created by governmental action in the creation of corporations and the grant of exclusive franchises. See Salter, *The Relation of a Municipality to Quasi-Public Corporations enjoying Municipal Franchises*, published in the Proceedings of the Baltimore Conference for Good City Government, 1896, pp. 219–225.

tained by government. In cities the maintenance of streets becomes one of the most important functions of the municipal authorities. A system of private highways, with tolls charged to all travellers, such as is even yet in use in many rural districts, would be absolutely intolerable in a city. Originally, when roads were built by the general government for military purposes, their maintenance was a secondary function. Now, both national and local roads and city streets are established and cared for with the direct purpose of facilitating private travel and giving opportunity for free transportation and change of place. But not only road-beds are provided. Street railways, ferries, cab lines, and other means are furnished for the conveyance of persons. Canals, express lines, and the postal service are provided for the transportation of things. The telephone and the telegraph are carriers of messages. Many or all of these services are undertaken directly or regulated by municipal corporations. From the nature of their functions it becomes necessary that common carriers and all public transportation companies should at least be under governmental regulation. One of the most urgent problems of modern politics in city, commonwealth, and nation is the protection of the public welfare in the matter of transportation. This protection is attempted through regulation and supervision, through ownership or through direct operation of transportation facilities. The municipalities of Great Britain have gone much further in the direction of municipal ownership and operation of street-car lines than have the American and French cities.

(*b*) A second group of common services of an economic nature, and semi-monopolistic, are rendered by government or under governmental control in the maintenance and management of terminals. First in this category are the piers, docks, wharves, etc., which are of so much importance to all cities with a water front. These terminals may or may not be owned by the city government. The great docks of London are owned by private companies. On the other hand, New York city, about 1870, entered upon a comprehensive policy for municipal ownership of the docks and piers on its water front. By the end of 1896 the city had incurred debt to the amount of $29,000,000 for dock improvement. Every city has its markets, which are terminals of commerce in food supplies and fuel. These are always under public regulation and generally owned by the city itself. Depots and warehouses are usually maintained in connection with the national customs administration. But Paris has its *entrepôts* or warehouses where products brought into the city for consumption are stored under the supervision of the *octroi* administration.[1]

[1] See Block and Pontich, *Administration de la Ville de Paris*, p. 200, and Chap. XLI., pp. 608–617.

(*c*) In the third place, government often maintains public institutions to which people may go for certain economic services. Important here are the municipal slaughter-houses of European cities. Public bacteriological and chemical laboratories also may render service to the individual aside from the direct protection of the public health. Many cities furnish public baths and lodging houses.[1] Some even maintain public wash-houses.

(*d*) Another economic service rendered by the government in great cities is the house-to-house distribution of domestic necessities. Even if this service is undertaken by a private corporation, the government must in many cases be called upon to grant the use of the streets for the construction of the machinery of distribution. This function includes the distribution of water, light, and heat. Water-works and gas and electric works are commonly maintained directly or regulated by municipal government. In America water-works are quite generally built and owned by the cities themselves. The magnificent supply of Croton water, first brought into New York city in 1842, has cost the city about $55,000,000, besides the expense of distribution within the city. San Francisco is supplied with water by private agen-

[1] See *Report on Public Baths and Public Comfort Stations*, published by the "Mayor's Committee," New York city, January, 1897.

cies. Detroit and a good many smaller cities have electric lighting plants. But Detroit does not supply electricity for private consumption. Many British and German cities own lighting plants for the supply of gas and electricity to private consumers as well as for public use. Manchester and the Scotch cities even rent gas stoves to the citizens. Philadelphia is the most important American city that has had experience in the municipal ownership of its gas supply.

(*e*) Lastly, cities are sometimes called upon to supply industrial necessities. Of the British cities at least Glasgow and Manchester furnish water and electric power to factories.

§ 18. **Idealistic functions.** — In the two paragraphs immediately preceding this, we have discussed what may be called the economic functions of government. They are not strictly necessary functions like those designated as protective. Whether any or all of these economic functions shall be undertaken or not, is in general a question of policy, to be decided by the conditions in each case. The real motive of government in undertaking any kind of business seems to be either the desire to distribute the burdens of government more justly, or the belief that public safety cannot be well protected if the business in question is left in private hands. In the two succeeding paragraphs we shall discuss a different class of activities, which may be called *idealistic* functions.

These are as socialistic, perhaps, as the preceding, and yet, with the rise of political democracy in the modern world, the encouragement of general education and the promotion of public morals by the suppression of vice have come to be regarded as essential and necessary features of governmental activity.

§ 19. **The encouragement of public education.** — Taking education in the broad sense, we may consider its promotion through several distinct means and in several different directions.

(*a*) Most important, of course, is the establishment or assistance of schools for general education. Universal education is a very recent product of civilization. It has been only about twenty-five years since a public school system was established in England. General public schools are usually under the direct management of municipal authorities. Professional schools are more generally maintained by private enterprise or by the central government. But technical schools are a very important feature of the public educational work done by European cities. Glasgow, Manchester, Birmingham, Oldham, Nottingham, Huddersfield, Paris, Lille, Marseilles, Milan, Hanover, and Chemnitz have established technical schools. In the United States something has been done for technical education by the cities. Boston opened its Mechanic Arts High School in 1893. Indianapolis has a Manual Training High School. New York city maintains a Nautical School.

(*b*) Another way in which general education is encouraged is by the maintenance of public libraries. This is an important part of municipal educational work. British cities have, in many cases, taken advantage of the Free Libraries Act, to the great benefit of the public. But Glasgow, so progressive in most things, has refused by popular vote to establish free municipal libraries. The great public library of New York was founded by private individuals and is under private corporate control. But the city has determined to furnish a site and construct a building for the housing of this library. The structure will cost about $2,500,000, according to the estimate of the law authorizing the expenditure. A great many American cities have established public libraries directly through the agencies of government.

(*c*) In the third place, the general diffusion of knowledge is promoted by the maintenance of educational collections of all kinds. These include botanical and zoölogical gardens, museums, art galleries, and industrial fairs and expositions. The fairs held by the mediæval cities were, perhaps, chiefly for the encouragement of trade, but they, like modern fairs, had an important educational influence.

(*d*) In some cases, finally, a city provides musical and theatrical exhibitions for the entertainment and education of its citizens. This function was most important in the cities of ancient Greece, but has not yet been entirely abandoned. Glasgow and Newcastle-on-Tyne, in Great Britain, furnish municipal concerts for which there is a small admission charge. In Odessa there is said to be a magnificent municipal theatre, and in Budapest one theatre is supported by the city, while one or two others are maintained by the general government. The city of Paris owns several theatres, which are rented to private persons the same as any other property.[1] Paris spends a good deal of money in the encouragement of the arts, even appropriating 70,000 francs a year for the promotion of horse-racing.[2]

§ 20. **The promotion of public morality.** — Morality is so bound up with religion that in these days, when church and state are separated, the government is greatly limited in its positive fulfilment of this function. It is true that virtue and the general precepts of moral conduct are supposed to be taught in the public schools, but in the main the political authorities depend upon the negative policy of suppressing vice. This is one of the most delicate tasks that government has ever assumed. There has been a great outcry against "sumptuary legislation" in the United States, and it is often remarked that people cannot be made "good" by law or police supervision. Many intelligent Americans oppose the policy of trying to suppress prosti-

---

[1] See Block and Pontich, *op. cit.*, p. 523.
[2] *Ibid.*, pp. 542–555.

tution, for instance. In many cities of the world, particularly in continental Europe, prostitution is licensed and regulated. The activities of the government for the promotion of good moral character may be summed up under the following heads:

(*a*) First, good citizenship is taught in public schools.

(*b*) Second, vice is suppressed by public authority. Here are included all those activities of the city government which are intended to prevent or put an end to drunkenness, prostitution, gambling, and kindred evils.

(*c*) Third, institutions are established for the reformation of criminals and the morally depraved. These institutions are usually maintained by private funds or by the central government, but may be established by cities also.

(*d*) Finally, the whole body of the law, both criminal and civil, is a powerful force in the establishment of moral ideals. Law is not only the result of general conviction on a particular subject. General conviction is often strengthened and crystallized by law. The system of private rights, as legally established, teaches self-restraint and social responsibility as well as personal freedom and self-development. The law of the family is a powerful agency in behalf of morality. The legal establishment of the family may, however, be regarded as a governmental function of an economic nature, undertaken to facilitate the transmission of property and to enforce parental responsibility for the care of offspring. But marriage is so intimately connected with the strongest moral convictions of modern society that we may regard the laws regulating it as intended primarily to promote public morality.

II. *Secondary Functions*

§ 21. Classification. — The secondary functions can be classified with even less precision than the primary functions. Strictly speaking, all those acts of government which are means to some further end, might be designated as secondary. But often the means is so directly associated with the end that an attempt to separate them would be quite scholastic. For instance, the construction and maintenance of sewers are so intimately connected with the disposal of sewage that for all practical purposes the means is merged in the end. But, on the other hand, sewage farms and the great establishments for the "reduction" of sewage and garbage may reasonably be separated as means from the general end, that is, the disposal of refuse. This end might be accomplished in other ways. It is possible, in spite of all the uncertainty and confusion in governmental functions, to distinguish broadly between primary and secondary functions, and to mark the principal lines which the latter take.

§ 22. To raise revenue for the maintenance of government. — The difficulty of distinguishing between the primary and the secondary functions of government is forcibly illustrated under this head. While it is true that government raises money only for its use in the accomplishment of the general public purposes, it is also true that we may regard the just distribution of the burdens of government as the primary purpose which determines between the several possible methods of raising revenue. Although the *burdens* of government are incident upon and secondary to its *benefits*, it is none the less true that these burdens cannot be escaped. If a city gets its revenue from property or business enterprises, the field of private initiative and private economic activity is just so far limited by the municipal policy. Something cannot be had for nothing. The burden of government is still a burden. It might, indeed, be argued that it is unwise for a government to undertake any kind of business by the profits of which the apparent burdens of the public service will be decreased. In democratic states the people who govern are likely to favor reckless expenditures on the part of government the moment the burdens seem to be lifted. It is the burden of government that most effectively maintains civic responsibility. The ideal system of raising revenue would make every citizen feel his share in the burden, and would convince him that he was bearing no more than his share. It is evident that, of the secondary functions of government, the raising of revenue is the most important. Without this all of the functions go unfulfilled. Revenue is the "wherewithal" of government. Revenue may be secured in several quite different ways. A private individual may earn money, or receive it as rent for real estate, or as interest on invested capital. He may borrow it. He may beg it, or receive it as a gift. Or, finally, he may steal it. The city, being a body corporate, may get money in all the ways open to the individual; and being a body politic, or a governmental agent, the city may also get money by means of taxation. An unjust tax is often called robbery. Taxation is different from theft by reason of its being legalized, and being undertaken by the agents of sovereign power and for the benefit of all. Taxation differs from theft not only in its sanction but also in its method. It is open, and it is not arbitrary. Taxes are supposed to be levied according to some uniform principle. We may group the methods of raising revenue for governmental purposes under the following heads:

(*a*) First, revenue may be got from property. This method of getting money for municipal expenses was much more important in the cities of the middle ages than it became later. Until the nineteenth century, modern cities were generally expected to support themselves by the revenues from their property, with the aid of certain tolls and receipts incident upon local police regulation. New York city, for example, did not get the permanent right to levy sufficient taxes for municipal purposes until about 1870. Up to that time the local tax law had been passed annually by the state legislature on petition of the city and county authorities. In British and European cities property is beginning to assume great importance again as a source of revenue. Budapest, Glasgow, and Birmingham are good illustrations of this fact. In Budapest the city owns large quantities of real estate, including some of the famous medicinal springs and baths. Glasgow has been making so much profit from its municipal investments that, according to a rumor widely circulated in this country, the corporation was not going to levy any taxes at all after the first of January, 1897. This report has been denied by the Lord Provost. The Glasgow rates for the year 1894–95 averaged a little more than four shillings in the pound sterling of rental value. This would be a rate of about one per centum on the full market value of real estate in an American city. Glasgow has, however, many municipal enterprises, such as tramways, water and gas works, and markets, which bring a net revenue into the city treasury. Birmingham occupies a noteworthy place among business municipal corporations chiefly on account of the great "Improvement Scheme," which will make that city the richest in the United Kingdom by the middle of the next century, when a large section of the city, covered with modern business structures, will revert to the corporation without cost. It is perhaps not very widely known that even New York, with its record of financial waste and mismanagement, receives a very large sum annually from its water-works, ferries, docks, markets, houses and lands, and other forms of corporate property. In 1896 the total receipts from these various sources amounted to more than $7,000,000.

(*b*) Second, loans are a source of revenue. This method of raising money is of great importance when costly public works are to be undertaken. Ultimately, of course, the loans must be paid out of the revenues derived from other sources. The power to borrow money is not a governmental prerogative, but is rendered very much more efficient when supplemented by the taxing power. In fact, the security on which most municipal loans are obtained is the sovereign power of taxation, rather than the mere possession of property or personal credit as in the case of private loans. The borrowing of money, for the purpose of making permanent public improvements, is justified on the theory that the burden should not all be borne by the taxpayers in a single year, when the benefits are to be enjoyed by the citizens for twenty or fifty years equally. It is often necessary also to borrow money for the payment of current expenses in anticipation of the collection of the year's taxes. For example, New York city does not begin to collect its taxes, for the expenses of the current year, until October 1st. This policy necessitated the issue of "revenue" or temporary bonds to the amount of $23,267,326.96 in the year 1896. Besides this amount borrowed in anticipation of current revenues, New York borrowed in 1896, $25,677,017.15. Probably Paris has the largest municipal debt of any city in the world. It amounts to nearly $400,000,000.

(*c*) In the third place, the acceptance of gifts and legacies may be a source of public revenue. This source is not generally of much relative importance for replenishing the public chest, but it may become important in particular cases. One of the chief reasons for making counties and towns municipal corporations in the United States was the desire to enable them to receive grants and execute trusts. Perhaps the most important gift to any American city so far has been the McDonough grant to New Orleans and Baltimore, by which the former city secured about $800,000 for school purposes.[1] It seems that gifts and grants in trust have been common with the older British municipal corporations. The City of London has become infamous throughout the world by the diversion of its endowment funds from the support of the needy

[1] See Howe, *Municipal History of New Orleans*, Johns Hopkins University Studies, Vol. VII., pp. 177-182.

to the entertainment of the rich.[1] Among the "mortification accounts" of the city of Dundee, Scotland, for 1895-96, we find some curious indications of the old-time faith in the *trust*-worthiness of municipal corporations. The following are examples: "HALYBURTON INSTITUTION, — the annual revenue to be distributed among three, four, or five maiden ladies in decayed circumstances," and "MRS. GIBSON'S BEQUEST for Annual Sermon to be preached against the sin of cruelty to animals."

(*d*) But after all, taxation, the fourth method of raising money for government, is the great resource of most cities at the present day. There are two distinct kinds of taxation. First, there are *general taxes*, which may be levied on persons, property, occupations, transportation, incomes, inheritances, etc. Berlin has an income tax, a dog tax, a rent tax, and a house tax. In the cities of the Southern commonwealths of the United States, taxes have been levied quite extensively on professions and businesses. In the French and Italian cities, "octroi" duties are levied upon commodities brought into the municipality. But in the great cities of America, the general property tax is the source of most of the municipal revenues, except for local improvements. Second, *special taxes* are levied upon real estate to pay for local improvements, such as paving, grading, and sewering

---

[1] See the book by Gilbert, *The City*.

streets, or laying out parks and boulevards.¹ In 1896, New York city collected $3,271,444.52 from benefit assessments. One of the important planks in the "London Programme" is the introduction of the "betterment tax," or special assessments. Most of the street improvements in American cities have been paid for in this way, and the London reformers are anxious to copy from us in order to bring about a more just distribution of burdens. Sometimes many difficulties are encountered in trying to put the system of special assessments into effect.² New York city suffered great losses under the "Tweed Ring," and for some years afterward through a defective assessment system.³ In ancient Athens special taxes were levied in the form of requisitions upon wealthy citizens to supply certain public services.⁴

(*e*) There is, finally, a good deal of revenue derived by cities from general police regulation. Here may be included receipts from fines and penalties, from licenses and permits, from franchises and official fees. Franchises might almost be

---

[1] For a full discussion of this kind of tax, see the monograph by Rosewater, *Special Assessments*, Columbia College Studies in History, Economics, and Public Law, Vol. I., No. 3.

[2] For the experience of Pittsburg, see an article by Mr. Geo. M. Guthrie, *Proceedings of the Baltimore Conference for Good City Government*, 1896, pp. 155 *et seq.*

[3] See E. Dana Durand's book, *The Finances of New York City*, soon to be published.

[4] See Fowler, *op. cit.*, pp. 173 *et seq.*

classed as municipal property. But when they are granted to private individuals, they are privileges, the exercise of which is subject to municipal regulation. In modern cities the value of street franchises has become enormous, and under efficient municipal government a large revenue is secured to the city from this source. In 1894 Paris received over $4,000,000 from its gas and transportation street franchises. There is a disposition in British and German cities to grant no important franchises in the streets, but for the municipal corporations themselves to undertake the public services required either directly or through their lessees. In other parts of Europe franchises are generally granted to private companies, but upon carefully planned conditions, usually including the payment of a substantial bonus and percentage of earnings. American cities have been very profligate in giving away franchises. The immensely valuable franchises of New York brought the city an income of only $263,176.52 in the year 1896, and that, too, when the citizens were paying a uniform five-cent street-car fare and $1.25 per thousand feet for illuminating gas. In Philadelphia, however, the street railway companies have been compelled to spend a large sum of money in recent years for the paving of the streets, which was a duty imposed upon the companies under the original grants of the franchises. The sum spent in this way is estimated at from

$9,000,000 to $14,000,000, the latter figure being the one set by the representative of the companies, while the former is an estimate by one of the city officers. Besides this, the city receives from the tax on dividends and the car tax about $180,000, and the state receives from taxes on capital stock and gross receipts something over $500,000.[1] In the modern city excise and other licenses also bring in a considerable revenue. Under the old excise license law of New York state, New York city received in the year 1895 the gross sum of $1,780,470 from liquor licenses, while Brooklyn received during the same year $882,350. During 1896, the "Raines Excise Law" being in force after May 1, the gross receipts of New York city alone from liquor taxes and licenses was $3,857,097.12.

§ 23. **To establish and maintain public works.** — The public works established by cities as means to the fulfilment of primary functions may be divided into two classes:

(*a*) Of first importance, perhaps, in the public works category are offices and buildings for the use of public officials and employees in discharging the primary functions of government. There may be included here city halls, fire-engine houses, police stations, prisons, almshouses, hospitals, schoolhouses, and buildings connected with all departments of the city government.

---

[1] See Speirs, *The Street Railway System of Philadelphia*, J. H. Univ. Studies, Fifteenth Series, pp. 53-72.

(*b*) In the second place, government establishes "plants" for the rendering of common services and for the better accomplishment of the primary functions. Here are included gas works, electric works, establishments for the reduction of sewage, sewage farms, filtration works, laboratories, etc.

§ 24. **To make public inspection.** — This function includes the getting of all kinds of information for the guidance of the government in the making and execution of administrative law.

(*a*) Of great importance here is the gathering of statistics. This work might have been classed with some propriety as a primary function for the encouragement of public education. But in so far as statistics are collected for the use of government itself, we have clearly a secondary function. Under this heading we may include, besides the taking of regular censuses and the tabulation of reports, the periodical assessment of property for purposes of taxation.

(*b*) A second item in this division is the inspection of food and drink products. It is easily seen that the concentration of population in cities, whereby the consumers of food products are far removed from the sources of supply and unable to protect themselves against the adulteration and contamination of their supplies, renders the intervention of the government to protect public health a matter of prime importance. It is by means of inspection that the public authorities get knowledge to guide them in their active guardianship of the public welfare. Milk inspection is one of the most important duties of a great city. British, French, and German cities have made much greater progress than most American cities in their system of food inspection.

(*c*) The inspection of buildings is an important form of the secondary function here being considered. Houses, factories, stores, theatres, etc., are inspected with reference to their stability, safety in case of fire, and sanitary condition. Building inspection has been put into the hands of a separate executive department of city government in some American cities. It is usually, however, connected with the fire service, the health department, or the general police administration. New York city and Brooklyn each have a commissioner or superintendent of buildings at the head of a department.

(*d*) It is also deemed necessary for government to inspect semi-public institutions regulated by law, but under the direct management of private persons. In this category are saloons, hotels, hospitals, private schools, banks, pawnshops, and other institutions in whose soundness the public is interested.

(*e*) Finally, the government is compelled to undertake a system of self-inspection in order to keep its parts balanced and in good working order. The auditing of accounts, the inspection of schools and public institutions, and special investigations undertaken from time to time, make this function important. The inspection of government itself is the most effective means available for enforcing official responsibility in a popular government. The city or the state, not being a natural person, cannot defend itself and look after its own interests directly. It has to trust a set of agents chosen in a more or less haphazard manner, and the only way to make them respect the common interests is to set them to watch each other or to insure that they may all be investigated by the people themselves.

§ 25. **To provide for the expression of the public will.** — By getting expressions of the public will, the government is guided in regard to the personnel and terms of office of its members, and in regard to the adoption of public policies and the execution of law. The expression of the public will in an organized way is one of the prime necessities of government in a country where the people are sovereign. It should be the constant and intelligent purpose of government to provide the best possible machinery for the orderly and prompt expression of the popular will. It is dangerous to the stability and sane administration of public policies, either to ignore public opinion, or to obey it as expressed through irresponsible channels, such as newspapers, partisan mass-meetings, the pulpit, and the stump. The organized expression of the public will may be made in two or three quite different ways.

(*a*) By means of elections the people choose their representatives to make and execute laws. Under the party system, an election means not only the choice of rulers, but generally, also, the choice of policies. The provision of elections is now universal in western countries, except in such anomalous cases as the city of Washington presents. That city is ruled by the United States Congress and commissioners appointed by the central government. The extent to which the elective principle is relied upon to provide an expression of the public will varies greatly in different parts of the world and at different times. The citizen of a Prussian city votes for one councillor every six years; the citizen of an English borough may vote for one councillor and one auditor every year, and in some cases for two revising assessors; while the citizens of San Francisco vote every second year for sixty or eighty different officers.[1] During the middle of this century, American states and cities applied the elective principle much more widely than before. The act to amend the charter of New York city, passed in 1849, provided for the election of the heads of the city executive departments by the people. It is now coming to be considered a necessary and

[1] See Moffett, *Suggestions on Government*, quoted by Professor Goodnow, in his *Municipal Problems*, p. 208.

F

wise policy, in American cities, to limit the number of elective officers so that the popular will may be more certainly and vigorously expressed in the choice of one, or a very few, responsible officers.

(*b*) In order to get an expression of the will of the people, the government sometimes refers projects to the electors for their adoption or rejection by general vote. It is quite common in American cities to submit the question of incurring debt for some particular purpose to the votes of the people. The question of consolidating New York city, Brooklyn, and their suburbs was referred to the citizens for an expression of their desires, at the election of 1894. In England, many acts are made to apply to particular cities only after the people have voted favorably. Glasgow, with all of its municipal progressiveness, has been prevented from adopting the "Free Libraries Act" by an adverse vote of the electors.

(*c*) A less formal and conclusive expression of the public will is obtained through hearings, petitions, and popular initiative. The right of petition is considered one of the fundamental rights of a free people. The new constitution of the state of New York, adopted in 1894, provides for public hearings on all special city legislation. The right of popular initiative is provided for in some of the Swiss cantons, and also in many American cities, in reference to certain subjects, such as local improvements and the extension of municipal boundaries.

§ 26. To represent the citizens in their corporate capacity. — Here are included all of those activities of the city government in its relations to the other grades of government and to individuals, which are undertaken to protect or further the interests of the municipal corporation.

(a) The authorities of the city government are often called on to represent the city before the central legislative body for the purpose of securing favorable legislation and defeating unfavorable measures. In the Brooklyn ordinances of 1850, among the various standing committees provided for is one on "Laws and Applications to the Legislature." In later years, when Hon. Seth Low was mayor of Brooklyn, one of his chief duties was to represent the city at Albany to protect his municipality from bad legislation.[1] The Cincinnati "Board of Legislation," which corresponds to the council of other cities, has a standing committee on "General Assembly." The Toronto, Canada, council has a standing committee on "Legislation and Reception"; and in Manchester, England, the "General Purposes" committee has a sub-committee on Parliamentary matters. It is thus no uncommon thing for a municipal council to maintain a standing committee for the express purpose

---

[1] See Bryce, *The American Commonwealth*, 2d ed., revised, Vol. I., Chap. LII.

of defending the city's corporate rights before the central legislature. In New York city it is said that the corporation counsel has to keep a representative at Albany constantly during legislative sessions, to protect the legal interests of the city.

(*b*) In countries where central administrative control is thoroughly developed, the municipal authorities have an important duty in representing the city in its relations with the central administration.

(*c*) Again, a city must often be officially represented in its relations with other municipal corporations for the purpose of making joint regulations or carrying on common enterprises. In the French Municipal Code provision is made for the union of several communes for certain purposes, such as the maintenance of almshouses, hospitals, and common roads and drains. New York city and Brooklyn have acted together in the construction and management of the famous "Brooklyn Bridge." This bridge is now in charge of a board of Bridge Trustees, appointed in part by each of the two cities.

(*d*) It is the duty of the public authorities, finally, to represent the city in the courts for the protection of its corporate rights and the prosecution of its legal claims against individuals. This function is of vast practical importance, as suits are constantly being brought against cities for compensation in the case of services rendered, or for damages in the case of the city's aggression or negligence. Here the city acts distinctly as a legal person dealing with other legal persons. This is also true in actions brought by the city for debt, for the removal of nuisances, for the expropriation of real estate, etc.

§ 27. Distribution of functions between central and local governments. — In this outline of the functions of government, with especial reference to the municipalities, it has not been possible to consider in detail the distribution of functions among the several grades of government. While the determination of what functions government in general shall undertake is not to any great extent a problem of political science, the distribution of functions among the various parts of the government is strictly a political question, a question of method. The method of the distribution of functions between local and central authorities is of extreme importance in its bearing upon the problems of governmental control. It is perfectly natural that the governing body of a locality, while exercising functions of interest chiefly to the citizens of the locality, should be responsible directly to the people themselves, rather than to the central governmental authority. But if a local officer is performing a function in which the people of the whole state are interested, the general government is held responsible and perforce must have the right to control the local officer. In countries like England and the United States, where most of the functions of government are performed by local officers, the control of the central government is in theory more absolute than is the case in the centralized systems of continental Europe. The difference is in the means provided for the exercise of this control.[1] In fact, the more thoroughly nationalized a state becomes, the more inevitable and resistless is the progress of central control over the local authorities. The circle of any particular function of government tends constantly to expand. New

[1] Professor Goodnow says, *Municipal Problems*, p. 86: "At the outset it must be noticed that the plan of a central administrative control which has been advocated does not in reality propose any further centralization than we now possess. There is now, and always has been, a central control over cities. It has been legislative; the plan proposed merely changes its character. It makes it administrative, but it makes it no more central than it has always been. . . . Further, it is to be remembered that central administrative control has, wherever it has worked most successfully, gone hand and hand with large local powers; and that it has nowhere been so far extended as to take from the localities subject to it, the power to decide for themselves their own affairs, — provided, of course, their decision did not involve the expenditure of so much money as to necessitate the imposition of high taxes, or to seriously mortgage the future. Therefore, central administrative control does not involve as great centralization as central legislative control, to which all American localities are practically now subject. The European method of regulating the relation of the localities with the central government involves, notwithstanding its central administrative control, a larger measure of home rule than is now accorded by the American method of regulating this relation."

functions, as a rule, are undertaken first by the localities. A striking illustration of this fact is seen in the case of the French communes of the middle ages. These little oath-bound communities developed the principles of civil liberty which afterwards became the possession of all France, and, though largely lost under the *Ancien Régime*, furnished the ideals of the Revolution, and are now the basic principles of every free government.[1] Unless experience demonstrates the futility of continuing any particular experiment in the domain of governmental functions, general interest is awakened, the function expands territorially, and finally the central government assumes control. There are, of course, necessary exceptions to this rule. But the complexity of city life makes it tolerably certain that the frontier of the realm of governmental functions will continue to be in the cities. The older functions will more and more be assumed by central officers, or brought under central control in some other way.

[1] See Dareste de la Chavanne, *op. cit.*, Vol. I., pp. 174, 175. He says: "Si multiple, si varié que fût son développement en moyen âge, l'administration municipale avait cependant portant un caractère commun. Partout elle établissait la liberté civile et la liberté politique. Quand elle perdit son indépendance, elle perdit aussi ce caractère; mais la liberté civile et la liberté politique ne périrent point pour cela; elles ne firent que changer de théâtre, et préparèrent en silence le jour de leur avénement définitif dans le gouvernement général du pays."

CHAPTER III

THE PROBLEMS OF CONTROL

§ 28. Sources of control. — The control over city authorities may be effected in two ways. Either the people through elections, petitions, the referendum, etc., exercise a control over the public officials directly, or the central government of the state exercises this control. In this outline, we shall discuss chiefly "central control," the restraining influence exercised by the officers and public authorities of a wider political unit over those of a narrower one. The two methods of control here mentioned correspond roughly to the double position of the city as an agent of the central government and as an organ for the satisfaction of local needs. This double position of the city is explained in detail by Professor Goodnow.[1] In a complete outline of the problems of government, the problem of control by the people directly would take a prominent place. This control, however, is not peculiar in any great measure to city government as opposed to general government. It is true that in cities changed conditions render the

[1] *Municipal Problems*, Chap. II.

problem of popular control more acute there than elsewhere. In so far as this is the case, we may discuss this intensified problem under the problems of organization; for organization after all includes the whole machinery of either central or popular control. In this chapter we are to discuss the relations of the city to the state. The city as a governmental unit may occupy one of three positions. It may be a city-state; it may be a grade of local government established by the state in the constitution; or it may be simply the creature and agent of the general government.

§ 29. **Forms of the city-state.** — Strictly speaking, the city-state is entirely independent of legal control, has no superior, and is limited only by its own will and the exigencies of international relations. If, however, we use the term "city-state" in a somewhat loose sense, we may distinguish historically several kinds of city-states, according to the degree of their independence. There have been absolutely independent cities, in so far as any political unit so far known can be independent. Then there have been cities in dependent alliance, nominally full-fledged states, but not such in reality. In the middle ages the feudal city often assumed the rôle of a city-state. And, finally, there have been a few cases in the world's history of cities which were members of a federal government, and could lay claim to statehood in the same sense that commonwealths of the United States can.

§ 30. The absolutely independent city. — No examples of the wholly independent city survive in the modern world; at least there are none in the world of which political science has taken cognizance. But Athens, Sparta, and Rome, in their prime, and other ancient cities belonged to this category. Venice of the middle ages was also a fully independent state.[1] But in all of these cases, time brought with it a departure from the true theory of the city-state. The city tended to become an empire city and exercise a lordship over other cities. In this way, the true balance and self-sufficiency of the city-state were impaired for both the dominant and the dependent city. The former developed into the empire and laid the basis for the modern national state. The latter gradually developed in the other direction, losing its autonomy, and finally becoming the modern municipal corporation. It is in this latter direction that we need to notice the changes in the city-state.

§ 31. The city in dependent alliance. — The first step in the municipalization of the city was taken when weak cities entered into friendly alliances with strong cities. Of course the weak soon became subject to the strong in many directions.

---

[1] See Henry Mann, *Ancient and Mediæval Republics*, Chaps. XXII. and XXIV.

Examples are to be found among the ancient cities under Athenian and Roman influence. Athens exercised a control over her allies in the Delian Confederacy that was little short of tyranny. In the functions of raising revenue, entering into foreign relations, administering justice, and framing a constitution, the allied cities were subject to Athenian interference.[1] Perhaps Sparta was even more disposed than Athens to dominate her allies.

§ 32. **The feudal city.** — The next step in the development of the municipality brought the feudal city. There were numberless examples of this more or less modified form of the city-state during the middle ages. Almost all of the cities of Europe were dependent upon some temporal or spiritual lord. The degree of dependence varied from almost complete helplessness to almost complete sovereignty. The allegiance of the great cities of northern Italy was merely nominal during much of the time. The Peace of Constance, negotiated in 1183, between the Lombards and the German emperor, Frederick Barbarossa, guaranteed many sovereign powers to Milan and its allies.[2] Of the treaty just mentioned, Mr. Mann says: "By that treaty the cities of the Lombard League were confirmed in the enjoyment of their regalian rights, both within their walls and the districts over which they exercised jurisdiction.

[1] Fowler, *op. cit.*, p. 288.
[2] See Henry Mann, *op. cit.*, Chaps. XIX. and XX.

They could maintain armies, levy war, erect fortifications, and administer civil and criminal justice. Consuls and other magistrates were to be nominated by the citizens, and receive the investiture of their offices from the imperial legate. The emperor was likewise authorized to appoint an officer in every city to hear appeals in civil causes. The Lombard League was confirmed, and the communes were permitted to renew it at their own discretion. Once in every ten years the Lombards were to take an oath of fidelity to the emperor, and they were required to contribute the customary provisions on the occasion of an imperial visit to Italy." Florence, Genoa, and other cities of northwestern Italy seem to have enjoyed a still greater degree of independence during certain periods. The middle ages formed a period of great confusion and uncertainty in the political constitution of Italy, but the tendency was always towards the *régime* of city-states. The cities of France and England also carried on private wars, made treaties, and regulated external trade.[1] Of the English cities Ashley says in his *Economic History* :[2] " Before the close of the middle ages, England was covered with a network of

---

[1] For the cities of southern France, see a series of articles by A. Ramalho, on " L'administration municipale en xiiie siècle dans les villes de consulat," published in Vols. LV. and LVI. (1896), of the *Revue Générale d'Administration*. Particular reference should be made to Vol. LV., pp. 407-409, and Vol. LVI., pp. 151-154.

[2] Part II., p. 94.

inter-municipal agreements to exempt the burgesses of the contracting towns from tolls when they came to trade; and these unquestionably led the way to more complete freedom. They are, indeed, almost the exact parallels, in that stage of economic development, to the international treaties of reciprocity by the aid of which many modern politicians expect to reach universal free trade. They began as early as the thirteenth century; Winchester and Southampton entered into such a contract in 1265, and Salisbury and Southampton in 1330; and they became more frequent as time went on." Mrs. J. R. Green, in discussing the political condition of mediæval English towns, says:[1] "The town of those earlier days in fact governed itself after the fashion of a little municipality. . . . The inhabitants defended their own territory, built and maintained their walls and towers, armed their own soldiers, trained them for service, and held reviews of their forces at appointed times. . . . In all concerns of trade they exercised the widest powers, and bargained and negotiated and made laws as nations do on a larger scale to-day. . . . The necessity of their assent and coöperation in greater commercial matters was so clearly recognized that when Henry the Seventh, in 1495, made a league of peace and free trade with Burgundy, the treaty was sent to all the chief towns in England, that

[1] *Town Life in the Fifteenth Century*, Vol. I., p. 1.

the mayor might affix to it the city seal, 'for equality and stableness of the matter.'" It should be said that the interference of the lord in the affairs of feudal cities was generally arbitrary, being determined more by the special conditions of relative power and mutual good will than by any settled principle of law.

§ 33. **The city a member of federal government.** — The cities of the Achæan League belonged to this category.[1] Indeed, at the present time we have the example of Hamburg, Bremen, and Lübeck, once old German free cities, now commonwealths of the new German Empire, subject to the control of the state through the federal constitution and the imperial government established by that instrument.[2] It is not necessary to go into the details of the control exercised over these three German cities, for that belongs primarily to a study of the relations between commonwealth and federal governments. The transition from this most attenuated form of city sovereignty to the next category is easy.

§ 34. **The city established in constitutional law as an agent of the state for local government.** — Under all its forms the city-state aspires to be

---

[1] Mann, *op. cit.*, pp. 119-121.

[2] See Burgess, *Political Science and Constitutional Law*, Vol. I., pp. 109, 124, 155-167, and Appendix II., *Verfassung des Deutschen Reichs;* and Vol. II., pp. 168-181, 264-292, 347-351.

something more than a locality, a municipal corporation. There are some cases, however, where the city is established by the constitution as a strictly local agent of the state. The complication brought into political theory by the existence of federal government makes it necessary to distinguish two cases: first, where the fundamental guarantees of municipal government are found in the national or supreme constitutional document, and, second, where they are found in the less uniform and more flexible state or commonwealth constitutions. The first case is practically of little importance. Yet municipal self-government is guaranteed by general provisions in the national constitutions of a few countries. This is true of Belgium,[1] The Netherlands,[2] Ecuador,[3] and, perhaps, some other countries.

§ 35. **The city in commonwealth constitutions.** — A general provision is made for municipal self-

---

[1] The constitution of Belgium, Art. 31, provides that "The interests which are exclusively communal or provincial shall be regulated by the regular communal or provincial councils according to the principles established by the constitution." These principles are laid down in the several sections of Art. 108.

[2] See Dr. L. de Hartog, *Das Staatsrecht des Königreichs der Niederlande*, a monograph published in Volume IV. of the *Handbuch des Oeffentlichen Rechts der Gegenwart in monographien*, edited by Dr. Heinrich Marquardsen.

[3] Art. 18, constitution of Ecuador, reads: "To attend to the interests of each locality, there shall be municipal corporations. The law shall provide for their organization, as well as for their functions and powers in everything concerning education and in-

government by the constitution of Honduras, which is now a member of the recently formed Greater Republic of Central America.[1] But it is in the United States that we find the most frequent examples of the establishment of municipal government in commonwealth constitutional law,[2] — unless, indeed, our theory of the indivisible state leads us to deny altogether the name "constitutional law" to the so-called constitutions of the commonwealths. At any rate, the cities that are protected by these instruments have in theory a more stable position than the city which is subject to the caprices of the regular state legislature. The con-

struction of the inhabitants of the locality, the police, the material improvements, the local taxation, the manner of collecting and disbursing the local revenues, the improvement of the public establishments, and all other objects within their jurisdiction."

[1] Art. 82 of the constitution of Honduras provides that "communities which have not less than 500 inhabitants may be incorporated as municipalities." Art. 83 declares that "The municipality is autonomous, and shall be represented by officers elected directly by the people. The number, conditions, and powers of the municipal officers shall be determined by a special law."

[2] For a general discussion of this subject, see Goodnow, *Municipal Home Rule*, pp. 56–98; and Wilcox, *Municipal Government in Michigan and Ohio*, Chap. I. See also the constitutions of the several states. For the older constitutions Poore's *Federal and State Constitutions* is the most available collection. For the constitutions as they stood on January 1, 1894, the *American Constitutions*, compiled for the use of the New York constitutional convention and published in its reports, is a very serviceable reference-book.

stitutional provisions of the states of this country, which affect the cities directly, are so numerous and so varied that it may be profitable to consider the chief subjects with which they deal. Indeed, in a federal government like ours, and in a country where the problem of municipal government is still so far from its solution, constitutional provisions for cities seem likely to play a more and more important part as time goes on.

§ 36. **Local choice of local officers.** — In the constitutions of several commonwealths the election of local officers by the people, or their appointment by the local authorities, has been required, or the state legislature has been forbidden to appoint commissions to conduct municipal business. It is interesting to note the difference in the provisions relating to the same subject in several constitutions. The New York constitution provides that, "All city, town, and village officers, whose election or appointment is not provided for by this constitution, shall be elected by the electors of such cities, towns, and villages, or of some division thereof, or appointed by such authorities thereof as the legislature shall designate for that purpose. All other officers whose election or appointment is not provided for by this constitution, and all officers whose offices may hereafter be created by law, shall be elected by the people, or appointed, as the legislature may direct."[1] This provision was first em-

[1] Art. X., sect. 2.

bodied in the New York constitution of 1846. The constitution of Michigan, adopted in 1850 and still in force, provides that "judicial officers of cities and villages shall be elected, and all other officers shall be elected or appointed at such time and in such manner as the legislature may direct."[1] These two provisions of the constitutions of New York and Michigan have been interpreted by the courts to mean quite different things.[2] And, oddly enough, the Michigan provision has proven a better guarantee of local self-government than the New York provision. Through the extreme jealousy of the Michigan Supreme Court on behalf of local self-government, the constitution has been interpreted as presupposing the system of municipal government in existence when the constitution of 1850 was adopted. Thus the benefit of the doubt is given to the people of the localities whenever the way of choosing local officers is in question. In New York, on the other hand, the Court of Appeals has given the benefit of the doubt to the state legislature whenever that body has attempted to regulate the choice of city officers. The Wisconsin constitution of 1848 copied word for word the provision first adopted in New York two

---

[1] Art. XV., sect. 14.
[2] See *People* vs. *Draper*, 15 N. Y. 532; *Metropolitan Board of Health* vs. *Heister*, 37 N. Y. 661; *People* vs. *Albertson*, 55 N. Y. 50; *Astor* vs. *The Mayor*, 62 N. Y. 367; *People* vs. *Hurlbut*, 24 Mich. 44; *Detroit Park Commissioners* vs. *The Common Council*, 28 Mich. 228.

years earlier.[1] But the Wisconsin courts have not had occasion to decide the exact questions involved in the Michigan and New York decisions. The Virginia constitution of 1850 provided that "All officers appertaining to the cities and other municipal corporations shall be elected by the qualified voters, or appointed by the constituted authorities of such cities or corporations, as may be prescribed by law."[2] In the present constitution of Virginia quite elaborate provisions are made for the election and duties of city and town officers.[3] The new constitution of Kentucky, adopted in 1890, likewise goes into considerable detail regarding the election or appointment of officers in cities and towns.[4] Another method of guaranteeing the local choice of local officers was adopted by the Pennsylvania constitutional convention of 1873. Provision was made that "the General Assembly shall not delegate to any special commission, private corporation or association, any power to make, supervise, or interfere with any municipal improvement, money, property, or effects, whether held in trust or otherwise, or to levy taxes or perform any municipal function whatever."[5] This section has been copied in its entirety by Colorado,[6] Montana,[7]

---

[1] Art. XIII., sect. 9.
[2] Art. VI., sect. 34.
[3] Art. VI., sects. 14-21.
[4] Sect. 160.
[5] Constitution, Art. III., sect. 20.
[6] Constitution of 1876, Art. V., sect. 35.
[7] Constitution of 1889, Art. V., sect. 36.

and Wyoming;[1] and, in an elaborated form, by California.[2]

§ 37. Formation of the charter by representatives of the city itself. — Missouri, California, and Washington have provided in their constitutions that cities of a given population may frame their own charters, subject to certain limitations.[3] Although this method of providing for home rule was first put into constitutional law by the Missouri convention of 1875, the practice seems to have originated in New York. In 1829, and again in 1846, there was a charter convention in New York city. The convention that sat in 1829 was called by the common council. Five delegates were chosen by the people in each of the fourteen wards; and the convention thus constituted drew up a new charter bill, which was submitted to the people, approved by them, and then enacted into law by the state legislature of 1830.[4] The city convention of 1846 was authorized by an act of the legislature. It was composed of thirty-six delegates from the eighteen wards, distributed roughly in accordance

---

[1] Constitution of 1889, Art. III., sect. 37.

[2] Constitution of 1879, Art. XI., sect. 13.

[3] A full account of these provisions and their practical working is given by Mr. E. P. Oberholzer, in an article called "Home Rule for American Cities," published in the *Annals of the American Academy*, Vol. III., pp. 736-763.

[4] See Chancellor Kent's book entitled *The Charter of the City of New York, with notes thereon*, etc., in which are published New York's Royal Charters, the Proceedings of the City Convention of 1829, and a treatise on the powers and duties of the mayor.

with population. The work of this convention was submitted to the people in November, 1846, and rejected by them.[1] Many of the proposed charter amendments, however, were incorporated in the acts of 1849 and 1853, which were passed by the legislature and approved by popular vote in the city. The published volume of proceedings of the city convention of 1846 contains many propositions and documents of great interest to the student of municipal government. One city convention has been held in Brooklyn also. It was authorized by a law of 1847.[2] Four delegates were to be chosen in each of the nine wards of the city. The revision of the charter adopted by the convention was to be submitted to the state legislature for its approval. The convention met on July 12, 1847, and finally adjourned on January 9, 1849. According to the act authorizing the convention, the revised charter was to be reported "to the legislature at its next session," which would be the session of 1848. The convention did not complete its work in 1848, and after the legislature of that year adjourned, many of the delegates withdrew from the convention, considering its further sessions and deliberations illegal. Nevertheless, a few of the delegates continued their labors, and prepared a revision of the charter for submission to the legislature. On the final

---

[1] See Durand, *op. cit.*, Chap. III.
[2] Laws of New York, 1847, Chap. 246.

vote in convention, only twelve of the thirty-six members were present and voting; eight being counted in the affirmative and four in the negative. Pressure was brought to bear upon the legislature, and the proposed charter was amended before being passed. The members from the rural wards had protested against the scheme of the convention to impose uniform taxes on all parts of the city.[1] These charter conventions in New York state, not being founded upon constitutional provisions, fell into disuse, and the state legislature, in its policy of interference with local government, has taken to itself the task of making charters. It should be mentioned, however, that the legislature of 1897 passed without amendment the Greater New York charter, as framed by a commission, appointed by the governor, from the residents of the locality. In San Francisco, where the city has been under the "consolidation act" since 1856, a new charter framed by a body of freeholders of the city chosen in accordance with the state constitution, was defeated at the polls in November, 1896. A modification of the home-rule plan in vogue in Missouri, California, and Washington has recently been embodied in the Minnesota constitution.[2] When villages in Min-

---

[1] See New York Assembly Documents, 1849, Vol. I., Nos. 28 and 32.

[2] See Durand, "Political and Municipal Legislation in 1896," *Annals of the American Academy*, Vol. IX., pp. 67, 68 (March, 1897).

nesota wish to be organized into cities, or when cities wish to be reorganized, the district court is to appoint a board of fifteen freeholders, who have been residents of the municipality for five years, to draw up a charter. This charter becomes law if adopted by a four-sevenths majority of the voters. The board is a permanent body, and charter amendments proposed by it require a three-fifths majority of the voters in order to be adopted. The legislature may enact general laws paramount to the local charters, but these laws must apply to all of any one class of cities. Cities are divided into three classes: those having more than 50,000 population, those having between 15,000 and 50,000, and those having less than 15,000. In the state of Louisiana, by an act of 1896, a majority of the property owners in any city or town may frame a charter and petition for its adoption. In that case an election must be held, and the charter becomes law if adopted by a majority vote. On the whole, it may be said that the grant to a city of the right to frame its own charter is an important guarantee of local self-government, if protected by a constitutional provision. This is true, even though the city remains subject to the general legislative power of the state.

§ 38. **The prohibition of special legislation affecting cities.** — A little more than half of the commonwealths of the United States require that cities be organized by general laws, or forbid the legislatures to pass any special laws affecting city charters. Ohio and Indiana inaugurated this policy in 1851. The states which at the present time prohibit special legislation for cities are the following: New Jersey, Pennsylvania, West Virginia, Kentucky, Ohio, Indiana, Illinois, Wisconsin, Minnesota, Iowa, Nebraska, Kansas, Missouri, Arkansas, Louisiana (except for the city of New Orleans), Mississippi, South Carolina, North Dakota, South Dakota, Wyoming, Utah, California, and Washington. The wording and effect of the provisions adopted in the several constitutions are considerably different, owing largely, so far as effect is concerned, to differences in judicial interpretations. The states not mentioned above which require the passage of general incorporation acts for cities are Virginia, Nevada, and Idaho. Texas prohibits special legislation for cities of less than 10,000 population. Florida requires a uniform system of municipal government except where special laws are in force. New York has a very important, though not a prohibitive provision to avert the evils of special legislation.[1] The cities of this state are divided into three classes by the constitution. Any act that applies to a single city or to less than all the cities of a class, is declared to be a special act. Every special act, after being passed by the legislature, must

[1] Constitution, Art. XII., sect. 2.

be submitted for approval to the mayor or to the mayor and council according as the city belongs to the first class, with a population of 250,000 or more, or to the second or third class, as the case may be. If approved by the municipal authorities, the act goes to the governor for his signature. If disapproved by the city, the act must be repassed by the legislature before it can go to the governor or become a law. All of these restrictions upon the action of the state legislatures are methods of governmental control rather than the direct guarantee of local autonomy.

§ 39. **Limitation of the financial powers of municipalities.** — Many of the state constitutions assert a direct control over the local corporations by fixing the maximum rate of indebtedness to be incurred or the maximum rate of taxation to be levied. New York, Maine, Missouri, and many other states furnish examples of this policy. New York limits municipal indebtedness, except for water supply, to ten per cent of the assessed valuation of real estate subject to taxation. The tax rate for city and county purposes in counties which contain a city of more than 100,000 inhabitants cannot exceed two per cent, not including sums raised to pay the interest and principal of the municipal debt. Maine limits municipal indebtedness to five per cent of the assessed valuation of the city or town. Missouri requires all municipal debts to be approved by a two-thirds vote of the electors, and limits the debt in any case to five per cent of the valuation. Other states whose constitutions limit municipal indebtedness either absolutely or subject to a special vote of the people are the following: California, Idaho, Washington, Montana, Utah, Wyoming, North Dakota, South Dakota, Iowa, Wisconsin, Illinois, Indiana, Kentucky, South Carolina, West Virginia, and Pennsylvania. The Utah provision is rather unique. By its terms, "Officers in counties, cities, and townships are prohibited from borrowing money in excess of taxes for the current year, except by the authority of the majority of the citizens therein who have paid a property tax for at least one year preceding." The rate of municipal taxation is limited by constitutional provisions in Alabama, Arkansas, Texas, Missouri, Kentucky, New York, and Wyoming. Cities are quite generally forbidden to loan their credit by the constitutions of the states.

§ 40. **Special provisions for particular cities.** — Some of the large cities are named in the state constitutions and specially provided for, particularly in the matter of municipal courts. New Orleans,[1] St. Louis,[2] Baltimore,[3] New York,[4] Brooklyn,[4] and

[1] Constitution of Louisiana, Arts. 128-147, and 253-255.

[2] Constitution of Missouri, Art. IX., sects. 20-25.

[3] Constitution of Maryland, Art. IV., sects. 27-39, and Art. XI., sects. 1-9.

[4] There is practically nothing in the present constitution of New York state which specially applies to New York city or Brooklyn.

Chicago[1] are so treated. But the last three are little more than mentioned for the sake of establishing certain courts in them. The framework of the city government of Baltimore is quite fully outlined in the Maryland constitution, although the provisions may be changed by the general assembly. The provisions for municipal government in the commonwealth constitutions of the United States are constantly becoming more varied and more specific. The attempts to guarantee home rule, enforce uniformity of organization, and limit local extravagance can hardly be said to have been thus far wholly successful. The city is, however, gaining an important foothold in what we may call our secondary constitutional law. The transition in our study from the city in this condition to the city in a state of complete dependence upon government is obvious.

§ 41. The city a creature and agent of the government itself. — With the full development of the modern state, the city has come to occupy chiefly the position of a mere municipal corporation, based upon ordinary statute, and controlled, altered, or abolished at the pleasure and convenience of the

---

An amendment to the constitution of 1821, Art. IV., sect. 10, provided specially in 1833 for the election of the mayors of New York. A constitutional amendment of 1880, Art. VI., sect. 12, provided for the organization of city courts in New York, Brooklyn, and Rochester.

[1] Constitution of Illinois, Art. VI., sects. 23, 25, 27, 28.

general government. In this category the city has no constitutional status, but is simply a local member of the central governmental system. This is the position usually occupied by municipal government in modern times. It is the obverse of the position held by Rome in the Empire. The imperial city and the municipal city lie at the two extremes. The city, as protected in its political rights by constitutional provisions, represents a reaction toward the middle ground from the extreme development of centralized government and municipal subordination. We shall now discuss the relations of the general government to the municipality as a subordinate unit. It is convenient to take up separately the sphere of control and the methods of control.

§ 42. **The sphere of central control.** — What acts of the local government shall be done under the supervision of the central authorities is determined, first, by the extent of the circle of interest in the performance of any given function, and second, by the distribution of functions between central and local officers. It has already been indicated that functions which are of general interest must inevitably come under the control of the general government. If such functions are performed directly by the central authorities, there is, of course, no occasion for central control over the local authorities. Thus it is stated that in the Hawaiian Republic there is no system of municipal government at all. "All parts of the country are under the central national government. . . . The Superintendent of Public Works and the Road Supervisors of the District of Honolulu are entrusted with the management of the roads and buildings. Health matters are regulated by the Board of Health; education by the Department of Education. The police are under the Marshal of the Republic. The Fire Department (paid) is a branch of the Department of the Interior."[1] Here, evidently, there is no opportunity for central supervision over local bodies. But under a system of "local self-administration," where local officers are used as agents of the central government, we find a central control, not only over the functions themselves, but over local officers who perform them. It is not possible to make a rigid outline of the sphere of central control; for this, like the sphere of governmental functions in general, is conditioned upon the caprice of time, place, and the public will. We may, however, indicate some of the principal directions in which the control of the central government has been generally developed.

§ 43. **Area and boundaries of the municipal corporation.** — A city, being primarily a body politic, must have territory. Residence is the most general basis of membership in a municipal corporation. It is readily seen that the question of area and boun-

---

[1] Quoted from a letter to the author from the *Foreign Office* of the Hawaiian Republic, dated 3d March, 1897.

daries becomes thus one of the most vital questions of municipal existence. In this field the central government usually maintains strict control. A city cannot ordinarily enlarge its boundaries of its own accord. In France the cities are communes, and a new commune cannot be erected except by virtue of a law passed by the French legislature.[1] A change of communal boundaries also requires the approval of the central government. In England and the United States, the most common method of incorporation or of extending municipal boundaries is by special act of the legislature; though in England the Crown in council may charter new boroughs, thus bringing them under the provisions of the municipal code.[2] In New Jersey a law of 1896 requires that a special act be passed authorizing the incorporation of any new municipality, although, once organized, it is subject to the general laws. In some parts of the United States the extension of boundaries, and even the original incorporation of cities and villages, are left to the action of courts or local administrative authorities, on petition of the inhabitants. Some such plan as this is necessary in states where special legislation for granting corporate powers is prohibited. In Ohio, for example, new corporations are formed after a petition has been presented

[1] French Municipal Code of 1884, Art. 5.
[2] See Shaw, *Municipal Government in Great Britain*, pp. 347, 348.

for that purpose, and a public hearing granted before the county commissioners.[1] A special election is held where a village wishes to become a city, or a city desires to advance from one class to another. Adjoining territory may be annexed to a municipal corporation on petition of a majority of the inhabitants with the consent of the council, or on petition of the council; and in either case by order of the county commissioners. The extension of boundaries attains first-rate importance when the population of a city has built up suburbs for residence or business. During a great part of the present century the city of Glasgow has been struggling to absorb its suburbs rather than allow itself to be surrounded and its growth and political development to be arrested by a ring of independent burghs. In his recent book on Glasgow, Sir James Bell says:[2] "Not only had the population overflowed the municipal bounds in various directions, but the overflow population began to crystallize into burghal communities on their own account, and since the middle of the century Glasgow saw forming around it a ring of suburban burghs, the existence of which almost barred the possibility of

[1] General Statutes of Ohio, sects. 1553-1571.
[2] *Glasgow: its Municipal Organization and Administration*, p. 54. This book is a large and interesting volume prepared by Sir James Bell, Lord Provost of Glasgow from 1892 to 1896, and Mr. James Paton, President of the Museums Association of the United Kingdom, published toward the end of 1896 by James Maclehose and Sons, Glasgow.

expansion on the part of the parent city." But in the long run the Glasgow corporation has succeeded in expanding its boundaries so that it is now in no danger of being throttled by its suburbs. The creation of Greater New York and of Greater Liverpool shows two recent examples of the importance of the problem of a city's boundaries. The improvement of a large area of semi-rural suburbs may be a great burden upon a city's finances. On the other hand, the annexation of suburbs, which are residence quarters for the wealthy, may relieve the financial difficulties of a city. In any case the general government keeps a close watch over the change of boundaries of the political subdivisions of the state.

§ 44. **Police administration.** — Of the functions usually undertaken by cities, the police service, including protection against fire, is one of the functions most often under the direct control of central officers. The general government of Prussia reserves the right to take over the police of any city when it sees fit.[1] In great capitals like Berlin,[2] Paris,[3] and London,[4] the police force is

---

[1] Goodnow, *Municipal Problems*, p. 100; *Comparative Administrative Law*, Vol. I., p. 330; Bornhak, *Geschichte des Preussischen Verwaltungsrechts*, Vol. III., p. 21.

[2] Shaw, *Municipal Government in Continental Europe*, p. 321; Pollard, *A Study in Municipal Government: the Corporation of Berlin*, pp. 145, 146.

[3] Shaw, *op. cit.*, pp. 35-45; Block and Pontich, *op. cit.*, pp. 69-81.

[4] Shaw, *Municipal Government in Great Britain*, p. 313.

directly under central authorities. In France the appointment of police officers is subject to the approval of representatives of the general government.[1] The local police systems of England are kept under control by means of a system of inspection and subsidies on the part of central officers.[2] In the United States police boards have been or are now appointed by the governors of the states for many of our large cities. Examples are New York (1857),[3] St. Louis (1861),[4] Detroit (1865),[5] Cincinnati (1876),[6] and Boston (1885).[7] A metropolitan fire board was established in 1865 for New York city and Brooklyn.[8]

§ 45. **Public health.** — In French cities the health administration is considered a part of the general police function, and so is kept under a strict central supervision as a matter of course.[9]

[1] French Municipal Code of 1884, sect. 103.

[2] See Maltbie, *English Local Government of To-day*, Columbia University Studies in History, Economics, and Public Law, Vol. IX., No. 1, Chap. IV.

[3] Laws of New York, 1857, Chap. 569, "An Act to establish a Metropolitan Police District, and to provide for the government thereof, passed April 15, 1857."

[4] Snow, *City Government of St. Louis*, in Johns Hopkins University Studies, 5th series, p. 166.

[5] Michigan Laws, 1865, pp. 99–115; see also Wilcox, *op. cit.*, pp. 109–111.

[6] Ohio Laws, Vol. 73, pp. 70–75.

[7] Matthews, *op. cit.*, p. 15; Massachusetts Statutes, 1885, Chap. 323.

[8] Laws of New York, 1865, Chap. 249.

[9] French Municipal Code of 1884, Art. 97.

In England a strong central control is exercised over the municipal sanitary authorities by the Local Government Board.[1] In the United States metropolitan boards of health have been established for some cities. New York and Brooklyn, in 1866, were put under a centrally appointed health board;[2] but this plan was abandoned a few years later. Detroit has at present a board of health appointed by the governor of Michigan.[3]

§ 46. **The administration of justice.** — In the middle ages many feudal cities administered justice with almost no restriction. Of course this was especially true of the semi-feudal cities of northern Italy. And yet, by the Peace of Constance, the German emperor maintained his ultimate jurisdiction in civil causes over the cities of the Lombard League.[4] In England the boroughs were generally subject to the final jurisdiction of the royal courts.[5] Yet the London city courts could try cases of high treason as well as the pettiest civil cases.[6] But in all modern countries the control of the central government has been

---

[1] See Maltbie, *op. cit.*, Chap. III.

[2] Laws of New York, 1866, Chap. 74.

[3] See Wilcox, *op. cit.*, p. 120; and Pingree, *Seventh Annual Message* as Mayor of Detroit, January 14, 1896, p. 13.

[4] See Henry Mann, *op. cit.*, pp. 420–421, and *supra*, p. 76.

[5] See Pollock and Maitland, *op. cit.*, Vol. I., pp. 627–635. For an account of the judicial powers of Prussian cities in the middle ages, see Bornhak, *op. cit.*, Vol. I., pp. 42–50, 149–153, 264–266.

[6] See *The Laws and Customs of London, op. cit.*

gradually tightening until now this field has been brought almost everywhere under central supervision. The principal corporation courts of New York city were abolished by the new state constitution of 1894.[1] Although municipal courts still exist in a special form in many cities, we can hardly find any not subject to the general governmental control. This control is generally exercised, aside from special legislation prescribing jurisdiction, organization, and procedure, by way of appeal to higher courts. In minor civil and criminal cases, however, the judgment of municipal, as of other local courts, is final. Possibly the courts of the City of London should be mentioned as being an exception to the rule of central control.

§ 47. **Public charity.** — Poor relief is administered under a pretty strong central control in England and France, and almost entirely independent of the regular municipal authorities. In England the system of central administrative control was introduced by the Poor Law Amendment Act of 1834. Poor relief is one of the functions that never devolved upon the English municipal borough, as such. Under the strict supervision of the Local Government Board, the relief work is carried on by the authorities of the parish and the union. In France the work of poor relief, so far as it is undertaken by the government at all,

[1] New York State Constitution, 1894, Art. VI., sect. 5.

is under a strict central control organized by *départements* or provinces. The actual relief work is carried on by the *bureaux de bienfaisance*, which are local bodies of the *communes* or of the *arrondissements*. A part of the members of these bodies are nominated by the municipal councils. In the United States there is a tendency to bring public charity under the general supervision of state commissioners and similar state officers. Amos G. Warner says:[1] "The first board for the supervision of charities was established in Massachusetts in 1863, and Ohio and New York followed with similar boards in 1869. We now (1893) have nineteen states with organizations of this character."

§ 48. Public education. — About the same degree of central control is exercised in public education as in public charities, though a considerably stronger control has developed in the United States. In England the borough councils have nothing to do with the ordinary elementary education. A separate school board is chosen by the electors, and the school administration is brought under central supervision by means of the Education Department, whose head is a responsible minister. In France the municipal authorities have a considerable control over the school finances, but the appointment of teachers and the general school administration is rigidly controlled by the

[1] *American Charities*, pp. 359–367.

central authorities. In nearly all of the American commonwealths there is a state superintendent of public instruction. His powers of control vary in the different commonwealths, but they are not usually very extensive. In Connecticut the enforcement of the compulsory attendance law has been put under the supervision of state officers.[1]

§ 49. **Finance.** — As long ago as the days of the Roman Empire it was often found necessary for the central government to appoint special commissioners to investigate the finances of particular cities or *municipia*.[2] In the later middle ages it was the extravagance of the French communes in contracting debts and disposing of their patrimony that led to some of the most important steps in the establishment of centralization under general laws, which reached its climax under Louis

---

[1] See W. C. Webster, "Recent Centralizing Tendencies in State Educational Administration," *Educational Review*, Vol. XIII., pp. 134-137 (February, 1897).

[2] See Arnold, *Roman Provincial Administration*, pp. 236, 237. The officers referred to were called *curatores rei publicæ*. Mr. Arnold says: "If the emperor wanted the accounts of any town to be reorganized, he appointed an extraordinary curator, generally a municipal citizen. . . . Being directly appointed by the emperor, the curators had naturally greater powers than the ordinary municipal magistrates; and as the local finances all over the Empire got more and more into a bad way, the old magistracies got less and less able to deal with them. . . . So the upshot is that originally curators were appointed by the emperor to meet some special need or distress of a municipality; and then little by little became regular and permanent magistrates. But they still were always appointed directly by the emperor."

XIV.[1] France, England, Prussia, and other countries now maintain a rigid central control over municipal taxation, indebtedness, and alienation of property.[2] In Victoria and New South Wales a system of special audit by appointees of the central government is in use.[3] In the United States also the control of the constitution and the laws is more marked in the field of finance than in almost any other. Of 1202 avowedly local and special acts affecting municipalities, passed by the Ohio legislature between 1876 and 1892, all but 78 dealt with local finance.[4]

§ 50. **Methods of control.** — Other fields of governmental activity besides those already mentioned may be brought under central control at the discretion of the general government. We have indicated simply the most important functions in

[1] See Dareste de la Chavanne, *op. cit.*, Vol. I., pp. 214-219; and Leber, *Pouvoir Municipal*, pp. 430-457.

[2] For France, see the Municipal Code of 1884, Title IV., Chaps. I. and III. The provisions of the Prussian system were contained in sects. 49-54 and 76-80 of *Städte Ordnung* of May 30, 1853. For the financial control exercised by the central administration over English boroughs, see the English Municipal Code of 1882, sects. 28, 106-109, 111, 112. For the canton of Geneva, and the city of Copenhagen, Denmark, see Ferron, *op. cit.*, pp. 228, 231. Reference should also be made to Goodnow, *Municipal Problems*, pp. 102-105, and Maltbie, *op. cit.*, Chaps. VI. and VII.

[3] See Jenks, *The Government of Victoria*, p. 364; and *Municipalities of New South Wales*, 1891, which is a reprint of "an act to establish municipalities, Dec. 23, 1867," and amendments thereto. See sect. 184 of the original act.

[4] See Wilcox, *op. cit.*, p. 79.

the exercise of which the local officers are often subject to administrative supervision. The field of control by legislation is as wide as the body of general laws affecting local administration and local functions. This brings us to a consideration of the methods of control. We are here considering only the control of the central government over the local authorities. The methods of this control may be differentiated according to the departments of government by which the control is exercised. We have the legislative, the judicial, and the administrative control.[1]

§ 51. **The legislative control.** — This method of control had its origin in the idea of the supremacy of law rather than of governmental officers. In England itself this method of control has, during the present century, yielded pretty largely to administrative control. It is still the principal method, however, in the United States and Canada. The control of the legislature over local affairs takes

[1] An exhaustive discussion of the methods of control over the administration in general is found in Professor Goodnow's work on *Comparative Administrative Law*, Vol. II., Bk. VI., pp. 135–302. Professor Goodnow has paid especial attention to the problems of control. These are the problems of municipal government which he had constantly in mind when writing his two other books, *Municipal Home Rule* and *Municipal Problems*. In writing the brief analysis of the methods of control contained in the text, I have had Professor Goodnow's work constantly in mind, and have made very liberal use of it. For facts and discussions relating to this part of the field, the reader should always refer to one or the other of his books.

the form of detailed legislation, usually of a special and local character. This method of control, when not supplemented by other methods, has proved inefficient as a check upon local extravagance, has rendered local responsibility impossible, has offered inducements for legislative carelessness and corruption, and has finally tended to degenerate into arbitrary interference with local autonomy.

§ 52. **The judicial control.** — This method of control also had its home in England. It is especially strong in that country and in the United States, where the judicial department is the final interpreter of the laws. This control may be exercised in one of two ways:

(*a*) By appeal, in the ordinary way, from local courts to general courts. Whenever the local courts are considered as integral parts of the city government proper, control by appeal may be considered as a judicial control.

(*b*) By the issue of the special writs of *quo warranto*, *mandamus*, *habeas corpus*, *certiorari*, *prohibition*, and *injunction*, and by ordinary suits in contract or tort. The courts maintain a very effective control over local officials by these means. Election contests are decided, officers are compelled to do their duty or restrained from doing wrong, administrative decisions are reviewed, and the municipal corporation is held to its responsibility as a legal person.

§ 53. The administrative control. — This method of control had its home in continental Europe, where it still remains practically supreme. It was introduced into England, beginning with 1834, to supplement the two methods already outlined. It has also been made use of in the Australian colonies,[1] and to a very limited extent even in the United States. The control over the municipal finances of the Roman Empire was administrative. There are several ways of exercising the administrative control. The principal ones are the appointment and removal of local officers, the issuance of instructions, the approval or disapproval of local by-laws, the hearing of appeals, and the grant of financial aid on the fulfilment of conditions.

§ 54. The appointment and removal of officers. — The appointment of local officers by central authorities, or even their nomination by such authorities subject to local approval, is a source of a powerful central control. The same is true of the suspension or removal of local officers. The governors of American commonwealths seldom possess these powers, although in a few cases they have authority to remove all or certain local offi-

---

[1] Professor Edward Jenks, in his *Government of Victoria*, already referred to, gives an interesting account of the local government of the colony and its relations to the general government, in Chaps. XXXVIII.–XLIII., pp. 325–365. The conditions in New South Wales are not much different from those in Victoria, so far as local administration is concerned.

cials for cause. Thus the charter of Greater New York provides that the governor of the state may remove the mayor of the city for cause.[1] The same provision has been in the New York city charter for about twenty-five years, and is contained in the charters of some other cities of the state, such as Yonkers and Poughkeepsie. The constitution of New York gives the governor the power to remove, for cause, county officers, including sheriffs, registers of deeds, county clerks, and district attornies.[2] This provision is copied, with a little modification, in the constitution of Wisconsin.[3] By a law of 1881 the governor of Minnesota was empowered to remove county treasurers in certain cases. The Florida constitution authorizes the governor to remove state and local officers with the consent of the Senate.[4] In Pennsylvania, "appointed officers, other than judges of the courts of record and the superintendent of public instruction, may be removed at the pleasure of the power by which they shall have been appointed. All officers elected by the people, except Governor, Lieutenant-governor, members of the General Assembly, and judges of the courts of record, learned in the law, shall be removed by the Governor for reasonable cause, after due notice and full hearing, on the address of two-thirds of the Senate."[5] The governor of Michigan has still

---

[1] Sect. 122. [2] Art. X., sect. 1. [3] Art. VI., sect. 4.
[4] Art. IV., sect. 15. [5] Constitution, Art. VI., sect. 4.

more important powers. He is authorized to remove all county officers appointed by him, and all county, township, village, and city officers elected by the people, " when he shall be satisfied by sufficient evidence submitted to him, as hereinafter provided, that such officer is incompetent to execute properly the duties of his office, or has been guilty of official misconduct, or of wilful neglect of duty, or of extortion, or habitual drunkenness, or has been convicted of being drunk, or whenever it shall appear by a certified copy of the judgment of a court of record of this state that such officer, after his election or appointment, shall have been convicted of a felony."[1] The exercise of this power by the governor is somewhat restricted, however, by the procedure required. Sworn charges have to be made to the governor, accompanied by a statement from the prosecuting attorney of the county that he thinks the case demands investigation. Governors of commonwealths have been given, in a good many cases, the power to appoint municipal boards or special commissions. In countries where central administrative control is fully developed, this power of appointment and removal plays a much more important rôle than in the United States. In France the central authorities have arbitrary power of removal over the mayors of the communes, and

[1] General Statutes (Howell's *Annotated Statutes of Michigan*), sect. 653.

may also dissolve the municipal councils. In Prussia the appointment of burgomasters in the principal cities is subject to the approval of the central government.

§ 55. **The issuance of instructions.** — Central officers often exercise their control over local officers by means of the sending out of instructions to govern official action. In New York the state Civil Service Board issues rules and regulations in accordance with which local civil service commissioners must act. The issuance of instructions is one of the most effective means used by the English Local Government Board to control the municipal administration. This is particularly true in matters of poor relief and public sanitation. In the more centralized administrative systems of Europe, this method of control assumes a correspondingly greater importance.

§ 56. **The approval or rejection of local by-laws and projects.** — The local authorities may be kept under control by being required to submit their plans to the central government for its approval. This means of central control is provided in a more or less efficient form in most or all of the leading countries except the United States. In France decisions and ordinances passed by a municipal council must be forwarded by the mayor to the sub-prefect within eight days. They may be set aside as illegal within thirty days by the prefect in the council of the prefecture. The commune may take an appeal to the Council of State at Paris. In England municipal by-laws do not go into force until forty days after copies of them have been sent to the Home Secretary, during which time they may be disallowed by Her Majesty in council. In Victoria any local by-law or ordinance can be annulled by the governor in council, and in New South Wales municipal ordinances go into effect only after they are approved by the governor and published in the government gazette. The laws of Prussia require the submission of some municipal ordinances, especially those embodying new financial measures, to a supervisory authority for approval. In the earlier charters of New York the common council was authorized to pass ordinances which would be in force first for three months only, and by a later charter for twelve months, if not confirmed by the governor and council. In France and Germany the approval of the central authorities is required chiefly as a guarantee that the municipalities shall not encroach upon the domain of the central government. In these countries the municipal corporation is put in charge of the affairs pertaining to the city by a general grant of power. The council is not limited by an enumeration of the subjects over which it has control. In cases of doubt, the presumption rests with the local authority. It is limited only by the general laws and administrative regulations or by specific prohibitions. The local ordinances are submitted to the representatives of the central government in order to have their legality determined. It is the province of the supervising authorities to keep the municipalities within their "competence."

§ 57. The hearing of appeals from the decisions of local authorities. — Sometimes where city officers have the right to act in the first instance, it is reserved to the central government to review their decisions. This method of control is strictly administrative when the appeal lies simply from an inferior to a superior officer. But in France and Germany special administrative courts have been established which furnish a semi-judicial control in lieu of the more strictly judicial control prevalent in the United States and England. The administrative courts are simply bodies of men connected with the active administration and skilled in the practical necessities of administrative law, who are given the task of deciding conflicts which arise between individuals and the officers of the government. The continental governments do not care to submit themselves to the legal control of an independent judiciary. In Prussia the Superior Administrative Court is an exception to this rule. Its judges are appointed for life and are not connected with the active administration. It seems that in practice the rights of the individual are amply protected by the administrative courts of Europe.

§ 58. **The grant of financial aid to the localities.**
— It is the history of government everywhere that control sooner or later gets into the hands of those who hold the purse-strings. It is a not uncommon thing for the central government to grant loans, subsidies, and endowments from the general treasury to the municipalities on certain conditions. This is one of the most formidable means of administrative control in the school systems of England and the American commonwealths. The system of granting state school moneys in aid of the public schools in cities and townships, on condition that the schools be maintained for a certain number of months in the year, is quite common in the United States. In England a rigid system of inspection is in force, by the results of which the grants in aid of elementary education are determined.[1] The subsidy grants are important in England for the control of municipal police also. But probably the subsidy system has attained its greatest importance in the Australian colonies. As recently as 1888, it was stated in the Sydney *Morning Herald Supplement*[2] that the various municipalities of New South Wales generally received more than £100,000 a year from the government of the colony, and between £20,000 and £30,000 from the ratepayers in the form of

[1] See Maltbie, *op. cit.*, Chap. V.
[2] A supplement to the *Herald*, published January 26, 1888, was called "Australian Settlement and Progress."

subscriptions to special works. Of the system of central control in Victoria, Professor Jenks writes:[1]

"In every important point the relation between the central and local authorities is that of master and servant. ...

"There are three principal ways by which the central government acts upon a local authority, viz.: by control of local legislation, by appointment of local officials, and by disposal of public funds. ...

"It is perhaps in the matter of public moneys that the central authority keeps the most effective control over the localities. The local authorities have always looked to the government at Melbourne for pecuniary assistance. From the days when it was attempted to force district councils into existence by a promise of a share in the crown land revenue, down to the wholesale endowment of municipalities in 1874, there has been a uniform system of subsidizing that has at length grown into a habit. But no less marked than the fact itself, has been the manner of its treatment. The municipalities have not been invested with the unalienated land within their limits, nor with the revenue from forests, rivers, or mines within their districts. It is true that they have been empowered to tax their constituents and to borrow money on their property. But a municipality which relies entirely upon its ordinary

[1] *The Government of Victoria*, pp. 363-365.

revenue is still a rarity, and the endowment which it obtains from the central authority is given in the most paternal way, by cash subsidy dependent upon the happening of certain conditions, as may be seen by any one who chooses to read the annual Appropriation Acts. Doubtless there have been good reasons for this practice, but its influence upon the municipalities has been very marked, in a want of public spirit, an absence of sense of responsibility, a hungering after a division of the spoil, and a feeling of dependence upon the central authority. It is, however, as the prime cause of the last effect, that we have to notice it here."

§ 59. **Central administrative control in the United States.**— In this country central control by the administrative authorities has had a very feeble development, and has been generally confined to charities, education, and justice, aside from the occasional appointment of police, health, park, and waterworks boards. The "Municipal Board Bill" presented to the New York legislature of 1896 marks an important advance in this general direction.[1] It seems likely that the United States will have to follow England and introduce administrative control over local authorities to supplement the legislative and judicial control so long de-

---

[1] See an article by Hon. F. W. Holls, "State Boards of Control," *Proceedings of the Baltimore Conference for Good City Government*, 1896, pp. 226–235.

pended upon to insure efficient local government. Whether with all three methods of control in use we shall succeed better in delimiting a "sphere of municipal home rule" than we have in the past is a question to be decided by experience. It is certain that French and German cities have a more substantial autonomy in local affairs than American cities have. It is also certain that British cities have gained in practical municipal independence since the introduction of administrative control. The essential problem of control, is, for us, the establishment of such governmental machinery that the sphere of the responsible actions of municipal governments will be delimited in political practice rather than in fundamental law. This brings us to the borders of the problems of organization.

CHAPTER IV

THE PROBLEMS OF ORGANIZATION

§ 60. Local importance of organization. — In the problems of organization we at last find a subject of distinctly local interest. The functions of municipal government are determined by the necessities of the environment, the spirit of the age, and the temper of each particular nation. The methods and extent of central control are fixed by the character of the central government and the development of national unity. But in organization, at least in its details, we always find the local spirit cropping out. It is the *how* of municipal government that is answered by each city for itself. Even under general legislation, providing a uniform charter for all the cities of a given class or of a particular state, the organization of administrative machinery must be left to a large extent in local hands. The almost exclusive problem of charter-framers for particular cities is organization. Functions and control are in general determined by forces that are continuous and cannot be greatly hindered or greatly assisted by the incompetence or the genius of charter-makers. The preponderant interest in the problems of organization shown by nearly all contributors to the recent "civic renaissance" in the United States, to use the phrase of Dr. William Howe Tolman,[1] tallies well with the real importance of the *forms* of local government. It is generally recognized that during the last few years a great deal more of active interest has been taken by "reformers" in our municipal government than had been the case in the period just preceding. The great local campaign in New York city in the autumn of 1894 sent a shock through almost all of our cities. Good government clubs, municipal leagues, and local improvement societies have been spreading everywhere. The national conferences for good city government have met every year since 1894. The movement for new city charters, however, did not begin with the struggle of 1894 in New York. Both before and since that time city after city has clamored for a "reform" charter, hoping thereby to reduce in some measure the evils of an irresponsible and inefficient government.[2] Despite the frequent protest that men are more important than

---

[1] See his little book on *Municipal Reform Movements in the United States*.

[2] At the dinner of the Minneapolis Conference for Good City Government, in 1895, Mr. Woodruff of Philadelphia said: "I was reminded, during my attendance at the conference, of a short piece of poetry I remember having read while at college. It described somewhat the state of my mind as I listened to the successive papers dealing with the varied forms of municipal government, — the coun-

measures municipal charter-making goes steadily on. It is necessary therefore to make a pretty careful analysis of the problems of organization. The first one of these problems is, of course, the basis of the suffrage; for the electorate is the widest category of municipal organization. Following this problem comes the division of the city into electoral and administrative districts. Then we are confronted by the organization of the government proper, the council, the head of the corporation, the administrative departments, and the city judiciary.

I. *The Electorate*

§ 61. The municipal electorate. — Every citizen that votes takes part in government. He must be organized into the general governmental system. The qualifications for suffrage furnish the basis of political organization. These qualifications are very different in different parts of the world. In some countries only a few have the right to vote; in others every adult male citizen

cil system, the board system, the representative system, the system of responsible heads, the federal system. The lines ran something like this:

"'The centipede was happy quite
Until a frog in fun
Said, " Pray, which leg comes after which?"
This raised its mind to such a pitch
It lay distracted in the ditch,
Considering how to run.'"

is an elector, if he has not forfeited his rights; and indeed in some cases women also have the suffrage. The requirements for voters in local elections, and regarding local affairs, are sometimes more and sometimes less exacting than for voters at general elections. The conditions of municipal suffrage may be best observed by a brief reference to the several qualifications upon which suffrage may depend.

§ 62. **Citizenship.** — The possession of citizenship in the country of which the municipality is a part is an almost universal qualification for local suffrage. But in some of the commonwealths of the United States, actual citizenship is not required, provided that the alien has declared his intention to become a citizen. The requirement of citizenship as a condition of municipal suffrage is much more important in the United States than in most other countries. A comparison of the percentages of foreign-born residents in some of the great cities of the world will illustrate this point very clearly. The foreign-born inhabitants number $2\frac{1}{2}$ per cent of all in London; 8 per cent in Paris; $1\frac{1}{3}$ per cent in Berlin; $42\frac{1}{4}$ per cent in New York; $35\frac{1}{4}$ per cent in Boston; $25\frac{3}{4}$ per cent in Philadelphia; 41 per cent in Chicago, and $42\frac{1}{2}$ per cent in San Francisco.[1] By the naturalization laws of the United States a foreigner may become a

[1] These figures are taken from the latest available census reports. Of course, the exact percentages change from year to year.

citizen after five years' residence, provided that he has "declared his intention" at least two years before taking out his final papers of naturalization. In the states where a foreign-born resident may vote during those two years, it may happen that a very considerable body of the electors are not yet citizens. The rapid immigration into the United States and the thronging of immigrants to the cities aggravate the case. There has been a considerable decrease in the proportion of foreign-born residing in the great American cities since 1860. This result is accounted for by the fact that children born in this country of foreign parents are reckoned in the census returns as native Americans. The naturalization of foreigners for immediate use as voters, has been a source of great political corruption in some of our cities. New York's experience has been particularly undesirable. During the Tweed *régime*, especially, the corrupt naturalization of foreigners was a great factor in elections. In an address prepared by a committee of the Citizens' Union, dated February 1, 1866, it was stated that the foreign voters of New York city numbered 77,475, while the native voters numbered only 51,500. In the Manual of the Common Council for 1860 the numbers of the native and of the naturalized voters were given as 46,113 and 42,704, respectively. The increase in the proportion of naturalized voters during the decade from 1860 to 1870 was in great measure due to the corrupt practices of the Tweed ring. The percentage of foreign-born of the total population of the city in 1860 was a little over 47. It must be remembered, however, that a larger proportion of foreign-born residents are adults than of native-born. If we were to count the native-born of foreign parents as really aliens, we should have had in 1890 less than 20 per cent of the residents of New York city full-fledged Americans. Conditions in Australian cities resemble those in American cities to some extent in so far as newness is concerned. In Victoria and New South Wales, it appears that actual citizenship is not required for the local electorate in cities.[1] Any one who is liable to be rated within a municipality, and who has paid his rates, is entitled to vote there. But aliens are not eligible to elective offices in New South Wales.

§ 63. **Residence.** — It is usually required that municipal voters must have been residents of the city where they vote for a certain length of time; though the ownership of property or the payment of taxes often give the right of suffrage without actual residence. In England property owners must reside within seven miles of the borough in order to vote there. In France, non-resident citizens may vote in the commune if they choose, provided that they have been inscribed there on the roll of one of the four direct taxes or of the

---

[1] See Jenks, *op. cit.*, pp. 330, 331; and Laws of New South Wales, 31 Victoria, No. 12, sects. 32 and 52.

road duty. In parts of Switzerland also actual residence within the municipality is not an indispensable qualification for suffrage. The length of municipal residence required is three years in Belgium, two years in Spain, six months in France, one month in Ontario, and different terms in other countries and in the states of the American Union. The term of residence required where residence is the determining factor in the suffrage becomes very important. A rapidly growing city may have its political welfare threatened not only by a great influx of foreign voters, but also by an influx of native voters from the rural districts. In order to be a competent citizen of a city a man must have become identified to a large extent with the city's special interests. As a matter of fact, however, the city probably gains as much from the intelligent votes of countrymen, newly arrived, as it loses from the votes of rustic "ne'er-do-wells" and "floaters." The requirement of a certain term of residence on the part of voters within the election precinct is of considerable importance in American cities. This requirement is made in the interest of honest elections to prevent "repeating," and is one of the incidents of the registration system. It is probable that previous residence in the precinct is made a part of electoral qualifications for the further purpose of disfranchising tramps and other citizens who are constantly "on the move." In a city like New York, however, where the population is so continuously shifting, many reputable citizens are likely to lose their votes by moving from the precinct within thirty days before an election.

§ 64. **Age.** — The qualification of age is usually the same for municipal and for national suffrage. In Belgium, however, a citizen must be thirty years old in order to vote at the communal elections, though at twenty-five he may vote for representatives in the lower house of the national legislature. Dr. Shaw gives an interesting account of the changes in the Belgian suffrage during this century.[1] The present electoral law was passed as recently as in 1895. Previous to that date there had been in force in Belgium a curious combination of tax and educational qualifications for suffrage. Persons who did not pay the amount of taxes required for voting might pass a special electoral examination. Professional men and persons holding positions of certain kinds were also allowed to vote. The age qualification was twenty-one years, instead of thirty, as at present. The age required for suffrage is in Switzerland, twenty years; in France, Italy, the United States, and the British Empire twenty-one years; in Holland, twenty-three years; in Austria, twenty-four years; in Prussia and Spain, twenty-five years.

§ 65. **Sex.** — Male sex is generally required as a qualification for voting, but in the English-speak-

[1] *Municipal Government in Continental Europe*, pp. 216–223.

ing world the suffrage is gradually being extended to women, especially to those who own property. In England women who are the heads of families or own property may vote in the municipal and parochial elections. Women have local suffrage also in Victoria and New South Wales, and full suffrage in New Zealand. In the United States woman suffrage is a question constantly agitated. Besides having the school suffrage in many states, women have full voting rights in Wyoming, Colorado, Utah, and Idaho. In Ontario provision is made for allowing all independent women to vote in local elections. Women have the same voting rights that men have in the municipalities of British Columbia. In most of these cases some property-holding or taxpaying qualification is attached, so that in practice few married women would have the suffrage. In the state of Kansas, where full municipal suffrage is granted to both sexes, we hear of women as mayors and other officials. It is not uncommon in the smaller towns in many states for women to be elected, chiefly by women's votes, to the board of education. The writer remembers particularly the case of Ypsilanti, a city of southern Michigan, where the women electors are often very active in campaigns for the choice of members of the board of education. Boston has in recent years witnessed a lively school campaign in which women took a prominent part. It is quite common now to have the school officers of the large cities appointed by the mayor, so that the voters, as such, have nothing to do directly with school matters. This is the case in New York and Brooklyn. In Philadelphia members of the board of public education are appointed by the court of common pleas. In the smaller cities and in the rural districts of many states women may vote for school officers. This is true in Massachusetts, New York, Michigan, Ohio, Illinois, Minnesota, Washington, and other states. No southern state has made any advances toward woman suffrage as far as the writer is aware.

§ 66. **Economic condition.** — This qualification is measured sometimes by the ownership of property, sometimes by income, and sometimes by the yearly rental of the premises occupied by the citizen for business or lodging purposes. The possession of a freehold is more often required for office-holding than for voting. It was a common thing in the earlier charters of American cities to require that the mayor and aldermen should be freeholders. This qualification still survives in some parts of the Union. The councilmen of Wilmington, Delaware, still have to be freeholders in the city. So also the members of the council in St. Louis. This is the case likewise in the municipalities of British Columbia. As late as 1804 only freeholders and "freemen" could vote in New York city for charter officers. By an act passed April 5, 1804, the New York legislature extended the suffrage in New York city to persons who had resided in the corporate limits for six months, and had rented a tenement of the annual value of $25.[1] The property and income qualifications are too varied to be outlined at all minutely here. The English lodgers' franchise and occupiers' franchise furnish good examples of the rental qualification. By the lodgers' franchise any man may vote who has, for twelve months prior to a certain fixed day of the year in which he wishes to vote, occupied lodgings in the borough of the annual value of £10, if let unfurnished. By the occupiers' franchise both men and women who have occupied premises for office, business, or residence purposes of the annual value of £10 may vote, if they have been rated for the support of the poor and have paid their rates. In the city of Dublin there were in the year 1896–97 only 8389 "municipal" voters, while in the parliamentary borough, which has less than 12 per cent more inhabitants, there were 36,193 parliamentary voters.[2] This difference was doubtless the result of the required qualifications for a municipal burgess, which include occupation, household residence within seven miles of the borough, and ratepaying.[3]

§ 67. **Taxpaying or contribution to the support of government.** — The discussion of taxpaying as

---

[1] See Kent, *op. cit.*, p. 127.
[2] See Dublin *Corporation Diary*, 1897, p. 52.
[3] *Ibid.*, *Standing Orders*, pp. 48, 49.

a legitimate qualification for suffrage would lead us far afield into the problem of the incidence of taxation. According to democratic theories it is not good policy to attempt to compel every citizen to contribute to the support of government in exact proportion to the benefits he derives from government; nor to measure the political power and responsibility of each citizen by the taxes he pays or the services he renders to the state. This general view is prevalent in the United States and most other republican countries. There is, however, more or less agitation to secure the limitation of the suffrage to taxpayers or property-owners, where questions relative to the expenditure of money are involved. This policy is actually carried out in many cases, such as voting school moneys or village taxes, and authorizing the issue of municipal bonds, or the levy of special taxes. The Evarts commission appointed by Governor Tilden in 1876, "to devise a plan for the government of cities in New York," reported in favor of a board of finance, to be elected by taxpayers and to have the general control of the finances.[1] Although having no advantage as voters, the taxpayers alone have the right to take part in the public hearings on the budget of New York city, and to force the investigation of official misconduct. But in monarchical governments there has generally been retained some form of the taxpaying

---

[1] See Bryce, *op. cit.*, Vol. I., pp. 609–615.

qualification for the ordinary municipal suffrage. As taxes are levied upon land and general property, this qualification is in practice intimately connected with the one described in the preceding paragraph. In Prussia and Austria the electors are divided into three classes, by different methods, according to the amount of taxes they pay. All of the classes have equal voting power. The Prussian system provides that all voters must be taxpayers. The list of the taxpayers is arranged with the names of the citizens in order, beginning with the one who pays the most taxes, and ending with the one who pays least. The total amount of taxes paid being divided by three, the taxpayers at the head of the list, whose quotas aggregate a third of the whole, form one class. Those next on the list who pay a third form a second class. The remaining names make up the third class. In Austria the three classes are made up of those who pay more or less than a certain fixed amount of taxes. Dr. Shaw tells us that at an election for councillors, in one-third of the districts of Berlin, in 1893, there were registered 111,637 men eligible to suffrage: 2045 in the first class, 13,049 in the second, and 96,543 in the third.[1] At Essen, where the Krupp gun works are situated, a recent registration showed four voters of the first class, 243 of the second, and 5367 of the third.[2]

[1] *Municipal Government in Continental Europe*, p. 307.
[2] *Ibid.*, p. 308.

The number of voters in the three classes in Vienna under the Austrian system is approximately 4500 in the first class, 14,500 in the second, and 41,000 in the third, according to Dr. Shaw's estimate.[1] In Victoria and New South Wales only ratepayers vote. Each elector has one or more votes, according to the relative amount of taxes he pays. In Victoria persons rated on property whose annual value is less than £50 have one vote each; if the property is rated at from £50 to £75, they get two votes each; and if the property is still more valuable, three votes each. In New South Wales there are four classes of voters instead of three. With property valued under £25 the ratepayer gets one vote; from £25 to £75, two votes; from £75 to £150, three votes; and above £150, four votes. The Sydney *Morning Herald Supplement* of January 26, 1888, stated that in the boroughs and municipal districts of New South Wales there were at that time 88,500 voters divided among the classes thus: with one vote, 46,666; with two votes, 28,388; with three votes, 8462; with four votes, 4954. It should be noted that in Stockholm, Sweden, every voter has a number of votes corresponding to the amount of taxes he pays, but limited to a maximum of 100.[2] In some countries the requirement of a taxpaying qualification operates to exclude only paupers, transients, and the most thriftless classes. This is

---

[1] *Municipal Government in Continental Europe*, p. 414.
[2] See Ferron, *op. cit.*, p. 233.

true particularly in England, Hamburg, and those American commonwealths which deny the suffrage to men who have not paid their poll tax. It is nearly true also in Prussia, where only a small percentage of the adult male citizens are excluded from voting. In Austria, on the other hand, only a small minority of the men are enfranchised.

§ 68. **Family condition.** — Sometimes householders are favored more than others in the voting qualifications. In Belgium heads of families who are above a certain age and who pay a certain minimum tax are given an extra vote. The householders' qualification in England gives heads of families an advantage, especially over their adult sons who are still living at home. The idea that the head of the family should represent all of the members of the family who still keep their residence in the household, is an inheritance from the old patriarchal *régime*. The modern world is coming to attach less and less importance to a man's family relations. Nowadays a man may become a full-fledged citizen before the law without having a family.

§ 69. **Education.** — The educational qualification for suffrage may take different forms. In Italy the illiterate are absolutely barred from voting.[1]

---

[1] See an article by J. H. Stallard, M.B., on "The Municipal Government of San Francisco," *Overland Monthly*, Vol. XXIX., pp. 48 *et seq.* (January, 1897). Mr. Stallard compares the franchise in the United States, England, and Italy.

This is the case also in some American commonwealths. Massachusetts, California, Mississippi, and South Carolina have an educational qualification for voters. In the latter two states a citizen cannot vote unless he is able to read a section of the constitution or to interpret it when read to him. The movement toward this kind of a voting qualification has gained a good deal of momentum in our southern commonwealths during the last few years. This scheme seemed to be the only way open for a successful restriction of negro suffrage without recourse to violence and intimidation. In Austria a preponderant influence is given to educated men, though in general suffrage is based on a taxpaying qualification. Dr. Shaw enumerates the following classes who are admitted to suffrage in Austria by virtue of their callings:[1] "(1) The clergy and all religious teachers; (2) high officials, active or retired, of the empire, the province, or the city; (3) military officers and certain others connected with the army; (4) lawyers, doctors, and pharmacists who have been duly graduated; (5) civil engineers, architects, and other graduates of technical and special high schools; (6) professors and schoolmasters of all ranks." In Hungary professional men are rated at double their actual taxes in making up the classes of citizens.[2]

[1] *Municipal Government in Continental Europe*, p. 413.
[2] *Ibid.*, p. 450.

§ 70. **Membership in extra-governmental organizations.** — This is the distinctly mediæval qualification for municipal suffrage, and at the present time hardly survives, save in the antiquated City of London, and to some extent in German cities like Hamburg and Bremen. In the City of London members of the "livery companies" are entitled to the suffrage because of that membership. In the mediæval cities political power was based very largely on the guild organizations, and citizens got their "freedom" by guild membership. This condition of things was due to the semi-private character of the mediæval city. It existed primarily, or at least the municipal corporation existed primarily, for the control of industrial and commercial activity. Only those persons who were responsibly related to industry and commerce by membership in the guilds could logically claim any share in the municipal organization and functions. Hamburg and Bremen are still distinctively commercial cities. Dr. Shaw, speaking of the Hamburg House of Burgesses, says:[1] "Half of the body, 80 members, is elected by the equal suffrage of all male taxpaying citizens. . . . 40 members are chosen by the ballots of the house-owners of the city of Hamburg, and 40 by a special electorate made up in a somewhat elaborate fashion of judges and some other specified dignitaries of state, and of the members of certain

[1] *Op. cit.*, p. 384.

guilds and corporate bodies." Of Bremen the same author says:[1] "Bremen's Bürgerschaft is a body of 150 members, of whom 14 are chosen by the class of citizens who have had a university education, — that is to say by the members of the learned professions, — 42 are chosen by the enrolled merchants, 22 are chosen by the mechanics and manufacturing employees, and the remaining 72 by all the other taxpayers of Bremen, most of whom are unskilled workmen."

§ 71. "Freedom." — Having the freedom of the city was also an important qualification for suffrage in the middle ages. The freedom of the city was obtained in mediæval times in many ways, as by birth, gift, purchase, marriage, and apprenticeship.[2] Under the Dongan charter only "freemen" had the right to trade or set up a shop in New York city, except at the time of fairs.[3] Among the privileges claimed for the freeman in the corporation's petition for this charter was the exclusive right to trade up the North River. The royal charters of New York city were essentially feudal and mediæval in their form and content, though no guild system was recognized. Municipal "freedom" is now of practically no importance in a discussion of suffrage, but the practice of granting municipal freedom to benefactors or distinguished

---

[1] *Municipal Government in Continental Europe*, p. 388.
[2] See J. R. Somers Vine, *English Municipal Institutions*, p. 37.
[3] See sect. 7 of the charter granted to New York city in 1686.

guests has not completely died out. It has already been mentioned that Dundee, Scotland, gave the freedom of the city to Hon. T. F. Bayard during the year 1895–96.[1] Glasgow has conferred the same honor upon Rt. Hon. A. J. Balfour, Lord Roberts, and Sir G. O. Trevelyan within the last few years.[2] The Roll of the Honorary Freedom of the City of Dublin since 1876 includes the names Rt. Hon. W. E. Gladstone, Ulysses S. Grant, Charles S. Parnell, John Dillon, Hon. Patrick A. Collins, Rt. Hon. John Morley, Cardinal Moran, Lady Sandhurst, and others.

§ 72. **Disqualifications for suffrage.** — There may be here and there other qualifications for the suffrage which have not been mentioned in the preceding paragraphs. If so, they are not of general importance, and could easily be given a place in the discussion of the suffrage in localities where they are found. But it is necessary to say a word about the disqualifications for voting. These are negative and exceptional in their effect, having for their purpose the disfranchisement of individuals, who by their special characteristics or actions are deemed unfit for the suffrage. There are numerous disqualifications in various countries, but the

---

[1] *Ante*, p. 18.
[2] See *Balance Sheet* of the Corporation of Glasgow, etc., 1893–94, p. 54; *Résumé of New Work*, 1892–93, p. 27; *Résumé of New Work*, 1895–96, p. 56; see also Bell and Paton, *Glasgow: its Municipal Organization and Administration*, p. 100.

most important are the holding of certain offices, the conviction of crime, and the receipt of public alms. The last is a disqualification in England and in most countries where universal suffrage has not been established. In the United States, paupers are often allowed to vote. The insane and inmates of public institutions may sometimes be disqualified for voting by law.

II. *The Division of the City into Districts*

§ 73. Civil divisions of the city.—Government must be organized with reference to population as well as with reference to territory. When a great mass of people live within a small district, it may be necessary to subdivide the district, in order to limit the number of citizens who are to act together in each local unit. In all cases where the people's representatives are chosen by districts, one or more sets of electoral divisions are necessary. And though the unity of administration, necessitated by density of population and the extension of governmental functions, may obliterate the township or parish lines, it cannot do away with the need of more or less permanent administrative divisions. Local self-government would, indeed, be an idle dream, if a great metropolis were to be congested into one homogeneous mass for governmental purposes.

§ 74. Electoral districts.— These are generally

subject to periodic revision in order to keep their population as nearly equal as possible for fairness in representation. Sometimes, however, equality of political rights is attained by changing the number of representatives from any particular district according to the increase or decrease in population. In Philadelphia each ward is entitled to one common councilman for every 2000 names on the completed Canvassers' List for the year when the election is to be held.[1] Sometimes the boundaries of electoral divisions acquire a certain rigidity, so that gross inequalities of representation take place. This is the case in the City of London, where there are 26 wards, each of which is represented by an alderman. One author says in regard to the wards of London:[2] "There are small wards and some large ones, but more small wards than large ones, so that a minority hold power. Some wards have been nearly absorbed for the sites of railway stations." By the census of 1871 Bassishaw ward contained 1006 inhabitants, while Farringdon Without had 20,846. Liverpool was suffering from a "rotten borough system" in its wards until its recent expansion into Greater Liverpool. Mr. Dolman, writing in 1895 before the change had come, said:[3] "There

---

[1] See Manual of Councils for 1896-97, p. 32.
[2] Gilbert, *op. cit.*, p. 210, quoting a writer in the *Westminster Review*.
[3] See *Municipalities at Work*, pp. 62, 63.

has been no extension of the city boundaries since the Municipal Corporations Act of 1835. Since that date, the whole of the available room in the city has been exhausted, even at the ratio of nearly 100 persons to the acre, and the population has overflowed into the outer districts to the number of about 150,000. These outer districts, to the extent of a population of 113,000 and an acreage of about 10,000, it is now proposed to amalgamate with the municipality. In the municipality itself, on the other hand, grave electoral anomalies have arisen in consequence of the shifting of population. Each of the sixteen wards returns three councillors; but whereas some of these wards have not 1000 electors, others have as many as 10,000, and in one case (Everton) as many as 25,000." Some twenty-five years ago Cincinnati had a very unequal distribution of its voters among the wards. Less than a third of the electors controlled a majority of the seats in the council. One ward had more than ten times as many as another.[1] In most American cities the wards are equally represented in the council, or at least in one of the houses, if the bicameral system is in use. The census of 1890 showed in every large American city, not counting New York, some one ward having a population anywhere from about twice to more than a

[1] See Debates of Ohio Constitutional Convention, 1873-74, Vol. I., p. 591.

dozen times as large as that of some other ward. This shows that great inequalities exist in the electoral power of the citizens, from the mathematical point of view at least. In New York city there are five sets of electoral divisions for the election of Congressmen, state senators, state assemblymen, aldermen, and judges of the district courts, respectively. The first three sets of divisions, especially, are subject to periodic rearrangement after each census. The electoral divisions of New York city for the several purposes have, in general, no relation to each other. The districts for the election of aldermen, however, are the same as the districts adopted after the census of 1890 for the election of assemblymen. The state constitution of 1894 increased the number of assemblymen so that the districts for their election had to be rearranged. The old districts were retained for the election of aldermen. At the present time there are 30 aldermanic districts and 35 assembly districts in the city. The wards ceased to be electoral divisions many years ago. The aldermen have not been chosen by wards since the charter of 1857 was enacted. In Paris each one of the 20 arrondissements is divided into four electoral districts for choosing members of the city council.[1] These districts ranged in population by the census of 1881 from 6975[2] to

[1] Block and Pontich, *op. cit.*, p. 81; and Shaw, *op. cit.*, p. 16.
[2] The quarter of *Santé* in the twelfth arrondissement.

72,324.[1] The electoral districts for members of Parliament and members of the county council of London ranged in population in 1891 between 37,705 in the City with its double representation and 113,244 in the Wandsworth borough.[2]

§ 75. **Administrative districts.** — In order to keep the administration in touch with the people, and to preserve as far as possible under urban conditions a healthy political localism in the various parts of a city, as well as for sheer convenience in administration, districts must be laid out and their boundaries respected for a moderate length of time at least. In Paris there are twenty such districts with permanent boundaries, each having its local centre of political and administrative activity. The arrondissements of Paris have their central municipal buildings in which the maires and their adjuncts superintend the administration of the schools, of public health and of charities, attend to the registry of vital statistics, make up the lists of voters and of young men liable to army service, etc. In 1881 the sixteenth arrondissement had a

---

[1] The quarter of *Clignancourt* in the eighteenth arrondissement. See Block and Pontich, *op. cit.*, p. 38.

[2] In the administrative county of London there are 29 Parliamentary boroughs, which are divided into 57 districts, including the City. Each district, except the City, elects one member of the House of Commons and two members of the county council. The City has double representation in both bodies. The figures for population may be found in the reports of the British census of 1891.

population of 62,876, while the twelfth had 213,128 inhabitants. The boundaries of these districts in the older part of the city have remained the same since the time of Napoleon I., and those of the newer districts since their annexation to the city in 1859. In Vienna are 19 similar districts. By the census of 1890 they ranged in population from 28,685 in Simmering to 158,374 in Leopoldstadt. Each of the 19 districts in Vienna has its locally elected board to look after its administrative interests.[1] London still keeps its old parishes and unions to the number of 42 for purposes of local administration. The great county of London is hardly more than an agglomeration of urban centres, which first developed their local life as distinct parishes or boroughs, and have since grown together by increase of population. Until the Local Government Act of 1894, the administration of parochial and district affairs in London was in the hands of vestries and district boards, which were practically close corporations, irresponsible to the people. But by the reorganization of parish government in 1894, the electorate was widened and parish councils were established directly responsible to the people. It is understood that local administration in London has been revitalized, and several thousands of Londoners are now actively participating in the local government as members of the various councils, boards, and

[1] See Shaw, *op. cit.*, pp. 417 *et seq.*

committees. The 22 wards of New York which are on Manhattan Island have kept their boundaries the same since 1853,[1] but their extreme divergence in population and the migratory habits of the citizens have made these wards entirely obsolete except as statistical divisions.[2] The last use of the wards of New York as administrative divisions, was done away with when the local boards of school trustees were abolished in 1896.[3] The wards are still used as United States census divisions and to a large extent as districts for the annual valuation of real estate by the city department of taxes and assessments. In 1890 the population of one ward was 929, while that of another was 245,046. These were the second and the twelfth wards, respectively. In 1895 their populations were 1034 and 364,412, respectively. By the census of 1860 the second ward, which was even then the least populous, had 2507 inhabitants, while the twelfth had 30,647. The most populous ward at that time was the seventeenth, whose inhabitants numbered 72,775. Besides the wards, there are

---

[1] See Laws of New York, 1853, Chap. 448. By this act the nineteenth ward was divided, and the western portions erected into the twenty-second ward.

[2] For light upon the shifting of the population, which is brought about by the encroachments of business enterprises and the rapid social evolution going on among the several groups of foreign-born inhabitants, the reader is referred to Mr. Jacob A. Riis' popular books, *The Children of the Poor*, Chap. II., and *How the Other Half Lives*.

[3] See Laws of New York, 1896, Chap. 387.

in New York under the various administrative departments about a score of different sets of districts. These include election precincts, police precincts, fire alarm districts, school inspection districts, dock districts, four different sets of districts under the board of health, five sets under the superintendent of buildings, street-cleaning districts, etc.

§ 76. **Principles governing the division of a city into districts.** — Confusion of the districts into which a city is divided has its cause in the three motives for the various divisions; namely, the desire to provide equal representation, the convenience of each particular branch of the administration, and the necessity of fostering local pride and local interest by maintaining permanent divisions. Wherever elections are by single districts, frequent changes in the boundaries of the districts are to be expected. Election by general ticket, or an occasional redistribution of representatives to the various districts according to the changes in population, would obviate the necessity of this instability of district boundaries. Divisions that are made for purposes of administration pure and simple, where the government always takes the initiative in dealing with the citizens, or simply manages its own affairs, may be changed from time to time as convenience demands without any serious confusion resulting. But in every department where the citizens of the localities have reason to approach the government of their own motion, it is highly expedient that district boundaries be as permanent as possible, and that the districts under the several departments coincide, or at least do not cut each other's boundaries. To expect any sort of local spirit and intelligent interest in the municipal administration on the part of the citizens of a city districted as New York is at present, would be preposterous. It is interesting to note changes that will be brought about by the advent of Greater New York. Of course, Congressional, state senatorial, and assembly districts will not be affected directly. The old ward divisions in the various parts of the greater city will remain substantially as at present. The most important change will be in the constitution of the five boroughs, — Manhattan, Brooklyn, The Bronx, Queens, and Richmond. Each of these boroughs will be an elective district for the choice of a borough president, and its boundaries will not be cut by those of the districts for the election of municipal assemblymen. The boroughs will each have their municipal buildings, and will in varying degrees be the centres of the administrative work of the several city departments. The charter commission, evidently, made a feeble attempt to copy the system of local divisions in vogue in London, Paris, and Vienna. Besides the districts for the election of the council, of which there are to be ten, and the districts for the election of aldermen, which are to coincide with state assembly districts, there are to be 22 "local improvement districts" coinciding with the present senatorial districts. The local improvement board, consisting of the president of the borough and the members of the municipal assembly residing within any particular district, seems to be a rather delusive organization, contrived to hold out the promise of popular local unity in administration. Of course, the subdivision of the borough into purely administrative districts for the use of the various departments is not attempted by the charter. That work is left to the judgment or the caprice of the future heads of departments. It should be noted that a really important localization of the public school administration in the several boroughs is provided by the charter. The first important step in the development of a lively locality spirit in a city is the establishment of districts for representation in the council. This brings us face to face with the problems of the organization and powers of the council of the municipality.

III. *The Council*

§ 77. The municipal council. — The importance of the council in city government varies greatly in Europe and America. In England, it is supreme, except as limited by the control of the central government. The supremacy of the council in the English system of municipal government is the most distinctive feature of that system, and has been commented on by many writers on municipal administration.¹ In Germany the council is a consenting, advising, and working administrative and legislative body. It is difficult for an American to comprehend the exact status of the German city council. It seems that the monarchic theory of the German imperial and state governments, by which it is the king or emperor who enacts laws, has had some effect upon the relation of the city executive to municipal legislation. In his excellent little treatise on *The Corporation of Berlin*, Mr. James Pollard, of Edinburgh, makes the following statements:² "There is a magistracy (*Magistrat*) of thirty members, chosen by the Town Council, but each magistrate must be approved by the Chief-President (*Ober-Präsident*), or Civil Governor, of the province of Brandenburg, who has his official residence in the city. The magistrates do not sit as members of council, but in a chamber of their own; and they alone have the power to initiate civic legislation, to elaborate its details, and finally to pass laws for the govern-

---

¹ See Shaw, *Municipal Government in Great Britain*, pp. 30, 63, 64; Goodnow, *Comparative Administrative Law*, Vol. II., p. 256; *ibid.*, *Municipal Problems*, p. 215. The English Municipal Code of 1882, sect. 10, provides that "The municipal corporation of a borough shall be capable of acting by the council of the borough, and the council shall exercise all powers vested in the corporation by this act or otherwise."

² P. 8.

ment of the city. The town council has no legislative functions, but may make representations to the magistracy on matters that seem to call for legislation. The latter body, if it approve, proceeds in the manner described with whatever measures may be needful to carry out the desired object." Further on, the same author says:[1] "Although the Magistracy and the Town Council in their corporate capacity act independently, and are somewhat in the relative positions of an upper and a lower house, yet, in the general work of administration which, as with us, is carried on by committees, the members mingle and have equal votes." It seems probable that this author was misled by the practical workings of the German system into the belief that legally the town council had no legislative power.[2] It appears that in law the council is the determining or legislative body, while the magistracy is the body charged with the execution of the council's projects. In case, however, the decisions of the council seem to be illegal, the magistracy may refuse to put them into execution pending an appeal to the supervisory provincial authorities. It is certainly true that the town councillors of a German city take an active and important part in the administration of municipal affairs through

[1] P. 9.
[2] The relative positions of the council and the magistracy are described by Leidig in his *Preussisches Stadtrecht*, pp. 100–107.

L

their coöperation with members of the magistracy and unofficial citizens on the departmental committees.[1] In France the council is almost entirely legislative in its functions. The French have undoubtedly carried the principle of the separation of powers further in the domain of local government than any other of the leading nations. The communal councils are so distinctively legislative bodies that the law prescribes for them four regular sessions a year, with the maximum length of each session. In practice, however, the Paris council, at least, sits very frequently, being in full session eighty or ninety times a year.[2] In the United States the municipal council has reached the lowest ebb of power. Here not only is it confined to legislative functions, as a rule, but even in the field of legislation the commonwealth legislature has assumed most of the important local functions. The tendency toward the distrust of American city councils has become so strong that in some cities the name "alderman" is an opprobrious title. A man's reputation would be smirched if you only knew that he was, or had been, an alderman. The corruption of city councils, and the consequent popular distrust of them, have led to a limitation of their powers in many directions. In the first place the system of the national and state governments, providing for

[1] See Leidig, *op. cit.*, pp. 141–145.
[2] See Block and Pontich, *op. cit.*, p. 82.

a separation of the administrative functions from the legislature, has been copied in the cities. In the second place the state legislatures themselves have assumed more and more to fulfil the local legislative functions of municipal councils. And, finally, in a great many cases, the powers of councils have been conferred upon specially created boards or independent administrative departments. The present common council of New York city is little more than a dummy of a local authority. There are many cases, however, in the smaller cities where the council still retains something of its old importance. The council system of government is still partially in operation in Minneapolis and Rochester, — cities with a population of between 100,000 and 200,000. But in the case of both these cities new charters are pending. A curious example of council government, or its obverse, may be found in the municipal history of New Orleans. By the charter of 1879 the "administrative system" was introduced into the New Orleans government. The mayor and seven administrators were elected by general ticket. The seven were at the heads of the departments of finance, commerce, improvements, assessments, police, public accounts, and waterworks and public buildings, respectively. Together with the mayor, these heads of administrative departments formed the council for local legislation. This system was superseded in 1882 by the more ordinary scheme of separate executive and legislative bodies.[1] Notwithstanding the weakening of most American city legislatures in the several ways already mentioned, the council may be considered, the world over, as the very core of municipal government. It will be necessary to consider separately its organization and its powers.

§ 78. **The organization of the council. Qualifications of members.** — Under the head of council organization are grouped all matters referring to the qualifications of councilmen, election areas, principle of representation, method of nomination, term of service, size of council, organization into chambers, methods of procedure, etc. The qualifications of councilmen may be as varied as the qualifications for the electorate. There is a tendency to require more stringent qualifications for the council than for the voters. In Hungary, outside of Budapest, half of the seats in the council are filled by those who pay the highest taxes. In Budapest itself, where the council is composed of 400 members, half of that number are chosen by the electors from the 1200 highest taxpayers.[2] In the city of Brooklyn aldermen are required to have been resident electors of the city for three years preceding

---

[1] See Howe, *Municipal History of New Orleans,* Johns Hopkins University Studies, Vol. VII., No. 4, pp. 17-19.

[2] Shaw, *op. cit.,* pp. 448, 450.

their election.[1] The members of the New Orleans council must have been citizens of the United States and of Louisiana, and residents of the city for five years prior to their election. They are also required to be 25 years of age.[2] In the early part of this century it was common in American cities to require that aldermen be freeholders. As regards residence, the policy of the United States is opposite that of England. In America the principle of local representation has got such a strong foothold that residence in the election area is almost always required of aspirants to elective office, including membership in the city council. In England any citizen with the required qualifications in other matters may be chosen to the council in any ward of a borough, if he lives within the borough or within fifteen miles of it. It is usual in some other countries, also, to allow non-resident property owners to be elected to the municipal council. This policy prevails in France, Victoria, and New South Wales. In Holland it seems that any citizen of voting age, whether he has the taxpaying qualifications requisite for voting or not, is eligible to a seat in the council. This is one of the curious instances where eligibility to suffrage is more restricted than eligibility to office.

[1] See Charter of Brooklyn, Laws of New York, 1888, Chap. 583, Title II., sect. 4.
[2] See Charter of New Orleans, sect. 9.

§ 79. The election areas. — The district forming the electoral unit is sometimes small, and sometimes as large as the city itself. The general principle of the French system is election by general ticket for the whole city, but in the larger municipalities districts may be established, from each of which several councillors are chosen on one ticket.[1] In various American cities the experiment of electing part of the members of the council by the city at large has been tried. For example, in Brooklyn, under that city's well-known model charter, out of a total of 19 councillors, seven were to be chosen at large.[2] This system was abandoned quite recently, and now 28 aldermen are chosen in seven districts, four in each. There are 32 wards in the city, and no two aldermen can be residents of the same ward.[3] Other American cities which have tried electing part of the council members at large are the following: Buffalo, where one-third of the members of the upper house, called the board of councilmen, are chosen by the whole body of electors every year; St. Louis, where the upper house, called the council, is elected by general ticket for four years; Detroit, where from 1881 to 1887, there was an upper house chosen by the people of the whole

---

[1] French Municipal Code of 1884, Arts. 11 and 12.

[2] See Charter, Laws of New York, 1883, Chap. 447; 1888, Chap. 583, Title II., sect. 3.

[3] Laws of New York, 1895, Chap. 976.

city; Louisville, where the board of aldermen is elected on general ticket; Omaha, where half of the council, until the new charter was passed in 1897, was elected at large every second year, while the other half was chosen by wards in the alternate years; Boston, where the upper house is composed of 12 members elected on general ticket with minority representation. This year's legislation, if accepted by the voters of Boston, will provide for a unicameral council, composed of one member from each ward and 12 elected at large, six of the latter being chosen each year. In Atlanta the six aldermen are elected at large, though chosen one from the residents of each ward.[1] In San Francisco the council is composed of 12 supervisors, elected on general ticket in the same way. The San Francisco school board is chosen in like manner.[2] The size of the election area is deemed of great importance in its effect upon the character of the representatives chosen. It is doubtless true that in American cities, where aldermen must be residents of their own wards, petty men represent petty districts.

§ 80. **The principle of representation.** — The principle at the basis of representation is influen-

---

[1] See Davis, "The Municipal Condition of Atlanta," *Proceedings of the Baltimore Conference for Good City Government*, 1896, pp. 96-101.

[2] See Milliken, "Municipal Condition of San Francisco," *Proceedings of the Minneapolis and Cleveland Conferences for Good City Government*, 1895, pp. 449-453.

tial in determining the size of the territorial unit of election. And yet there may be different principles of representation used in the case of like election areas. The English system provides general representation. There the local body of electors acts as an agent of the whole community for the choice of representatives of the whole community. Residence in a local area is not required of a representative chosen by the electors of that area. In the United States, on the other hand, local residence is required in most cases. This gives us the system of local representation as opposed to general representation. The plan adopted in the United States is a part of the general scheme of local self-government. Besides the principles of representation which have their basis in residence, there are numerous other principles in use. It will be necessary to take these up separately in succeeding sections.

§ 81. Minority representation. — This is the principle in force where no voter is allowed to vote for more than a certain proportion of councilmen to be elected in the election area, or where any voter may cumulate his votes on one or more candidates. In Boston a law of 1893 required that no elector should vote for more than seven of the 12 aldermen to be chosen. In New York city from 1873 to 1882 no elector was permitted to vote for more than two-thirds of the members of council chosen at large and two-thirds of those elected in his "senate district." The Boston scheme turned out to be a more galling collar on the neck of the independent voter than the old system of simple election by plurality of votes. For under the new system each party nominated only seven candidates, and 12 of the 14 thus put up by the two leading parties were sure of election, leaving only two names to be rejected by the voters who were insubordinate to the party machines! Under the old scheme, on the other hand, 24 men were nominated for the 12 places, and 12 names had to be rejected. The charter of Bridgeport, Conn., passed in 1895, has a very peculiar provision for minority representation. Ten aldermen are to be elected every year. Each party is to nominate and place on its ticket a full list of 10 names. Section 12 of the charter goes on to provide as follows: "The secretary of the meeting of each political party nominating candidates for aldermen shall file in the office of the town clerk a list, by him attested and signed, of the aldermen nominated by such party, at least thirty-six hours before the opening of the polls on election day. In case any party shall fail to nominate the number of candidates for aldermen herein required to be nominated, or in case any such secretary shall fail to file such list, the ballots cast for candidates for aldermen of such party shall not be counted. But nothing herein contained shall be construed so as to prevent any voter from erasing any name from a ticket to be voted, or from inserting in place of any name the name of any other person. Any number of voters associated together, and nominating candidates for town or city offices, either directly or through a convention to which delegates shall be chosen, shall be a political party within the meaning of this act." The next section provides that the two parties receiving the highest and the next highest votes for all 10 aldermen shall each be entitled to five. As between the candidates of the same party a plurality of votes is to decide, or if there is a tie, then priority on the nomination list. The five candidates of each party not elected go upon an eligible list in the order of the number of votes received, and are taken in that order to fill vacancies in their party's representation in the council. It appears that under this Bridgeport scheme an independent voter can vote for five candidates of one party and then give his preference for five candidates of the other party also. At least, it appears that the law is so interpreted in practice. Thus the whole body of citizens is given an opportunity to choose five out of 10 candidates put in the field by each of the two principal parties. Good citizens of both parties can coöperate to elect the best candidates. The professional politicians can coöperate for a different purpose. The usual rule under minority representation is that the requisite number of candidates having the highest votes are elected. But

New York city has experimented with a peculiar scheme for representing the minority party. On two or three occasions laws have been enacted establishing boards of, say, twelve members to be elected at large, of whom no more than six or seven could be voted for on the same ticket. The six or seven receiving the highest votes were to be elected and the six or five receiving the next highest votes were to be appointed by the mayor. A law of 1849 provided for a board of ten "governors of the almshouse." One governor was to be elected annually, for a term of five years, and the candidate receiving the next highest vote to the one elected was to be appointed by the mayor.[1] An act of 1857 provided for a board of twelve supervisors to be chosen annually. Six were to be elected, and the six having the next highest votes were to be appointed.[2] The same principle was extended by an act of 1869 to the board of education, except that seven commissioners were to be elected and five appointed.[3] The cumulative system of voting has been tried in the election of school boards in England, and of members of the legislature in the state of Illinois. The experi-

[1] Laws of New York, 1849, Chap. 246, "An act to provide for the government of the department of alms and penitentiary in the city and county of New York."

[2] Laws of New York, 1857, Chap. 590, "An act relating to the board of supervisors of the county of New York."

[3] Laws of New York, 1869, Chap. 437, "An act relative to common schools in the city of New York."

ment in both places has not been wholly satisfactory.[1]

§ 82. Proportional representation. — This is the principle in use where each party elects a number of councilmen in accordance with the proportion of the total vote cast by the members of that party. Various schemes of proportional representation have been elaborated by theorists, and some practical experiments have been made in European countries, particularly in Switzerland and Belgium.[2] There seems to be considerable difference of opinion as to whether or not the satisfactory workableness of this scheme has as yet been demonstrated.[3] Some reformers claim that the workableness of proportional representation has been proven beyond a doubt, while men like Professor Goodnow see practical difficulties still to be overcome. The most telling objection urged against minority and proportional representation is that they render a party machine and party discipline still more necessary than they are at present, and so diminish the power of the independent voter. The tendency of the movement for proportional representation is

---

[1] See Goodnow, *Municipal Problems*, pp. 154-156.

[2] For a discussion of the whole problem, see Professor J. R. Commons' book, *Proportional Representation*. References to the experiments in Belgium and Switzerland are found on pp. 122-131, 239-242. An interesting review of this book appeared from Professor Goodnow's pen in the *Political Science Quarterly*, Vol. XI. (1896), pp. 551-553.

[3] See Goodnow, *Municipal Problems*, pp. 154-179.

toward the destruction of the bi-partisan system of government, and the substitution of representative democracy for the existing republicanism of political institutions.

§ 83. **Class representation.** — The cities of Hamburg and Bremen have quite elaborate systems of class representation in the election of their governing council, by which the merchants, the householders, the workingmen, etc., have their own selected representatives.[1] In Prussia and Austria there are three classes of voters, based upon wealth as shown by the amount of taxes they pay.[2] Each class elects its own members of the council.

§ 84. **Methods of nomination.** — There are two principal systems of effecting the nomination of candidates for the office of municipal councilman. In the United States, and perhaps also in France, the political parties hold caucuses or nominating conventions or primaries, as they are variously called, for the choice of party candidates. This system is incident to the control of municipal affairs by national political parties. In England it is provided that any two electors of a given ward may propose and second and, with the assistance of eight others, effect the legal nomination of any eligible person as a candidate for a seat in the municipal council.[3] If there are no more nomina-

---

[1] Shaw, *op. cit.*, pp. 384, 388.   [2] *Ante*, p. 127.
[3] English Municipal Code of 1882, sects. 55, 56.

tions than places to be filled, no vote is taken, but the nominees are declared elected. This system, with some modifications, prevails in Great Britain, Ontario, Victoria, New South Wales, British Columbia, and probably other parts of the British dominion. The system of nominations for members of the municipal council developed in Great Britain and the colonies is so interesting that some further account of it should be given here. In England the nominations must be made at least seven days before the day of election. The town clerk sends notice to each candidate, giving a list of all the candidates. On the following day, six days before the poll, the mayor has a hearing to determine on the legality of the various nominations. At least four days before election the town clerk posts a corrected list of the nominees, with their "description," and the names of their proposers and seconders. After this any candidate is allowed to withdraw, if he desires, until the number of candidates does not exceed the number of vacancies to be filled. Service is compulsory, and if no nominations at all are made, the retiring councillors are declared reëlected. In Glasgow the candidate himself must sign his nomination paper. The signatures of a proposer, a seconder, and five other registered electors are required for a valid nomination. The same general system, with minor variations, is in use in all the Royal Burghs of

Scotland.[1] In Victoria nomination papers must be signed by ten electors and by the candidate himself, to show his willingness to stand as a candidate. These papers are filed with the returning officer, and in each case the sum of £10 must be deposited. This money goes to help pay the official expenses of the election, if the candidate fails to get one-fifth as many votes as the last person on the list who is elected. Up to four days before the election, a candidate may retire and withdraw his deposit, if he can get the consent of half of his ten nominators.[2] The municipal law of New South Wales[3] requires that nominations be made in writing, signed by two electors, and delivered to the clerk at least seven days before the election. On the "day of nomination" the names of the nominees and their proposers, with their description and qualifications as electors, are publicly read. If there are no more nominees than places to be filled, they are declared elected. Otherwise there is a poll. But any person nominated may by written notice withdraw at any time before the day of nomination. Service, after election, is compulsory. In Ontario the nomination system is still further modified. A public meeting of the electors is held on the last Monday in December of each year, after six days' notice. The

---

[1] See Bell and Paton, *op. cit.*, pp. 67-69.
[2] See Jenks, *op. cit.*, p. 332.
[3] Sect. 66.

returning officer presides and nominations are in order. If, after one hour's time, no more candidates are named than one for each of the places vacant, they are declared elected. Otherwise, provided a poll is demanded, an election is held on the first day of January following. By the law of 1866 every candidate had a column in the poll-book, and in it was placed the figure "1" opposite the name of every voter who voted for him. Elections are now by ballot, according to the terms of the municipal act. The Municipal Elections Act of British Columbia, passed April 17, 1896, provides that nominations must be in writing signed by two electors, accompanied by the written consent of the candidate to his nomination. Notice of the election must be published at least six days before the day of nomination. Nominations will be received till two o'clock in the afternoon of that day. If a poll is necessary the proceedings will be adjourned to the election day named in the notice. A candidate may withdraw at any time before the day preceding the poll.

§ 85. **Term of service.** — The length of time for which municipal councillors are chosen is determined mainly by two considerations: the desire to maintain an active popular control, and the desire to have an experienced and capable council. The actual policy in regard to the terms of service is usually the result of a compromise between these two desires. It is quite common to provide for experience in the council by the system of partial renewal. There is, however, no sort of agreement in the various countries of the world on the general question. London elects the whole body of its councillors, not including the 19 aldermen, at the end of every three years. In other English cities, as well as in Australian and Canadian cities, one-third of the council is chosen every year. French councils retire in a body at the end of four years, and Hungarian councils at the end of six. In Prussia, Austria, and Holland councils are chosen by thirds every two years. In Hamburg and Belgian cities they are chosen by halves every three years. In Italy one-fifth of the councillors are chosen every second year. The practice of American cities is extremely varied, though the term of office is seldom, if ever, more than four years.

§ 86. **Size of council.** — In Europe councils are generally larger than in America. London has about 140 councillors; Manchester, 104; Glasgow, 77; Paris, 80; Berlin, 126; Vienna, 138; and Budapest, 400; New York city has 31 councilmen; Brooklyn, 28; Cleveland, 22; Chicago, 68; Philadelphia, 170; St. Louis, 41; Boston, 87; Providence, 50; and San Francisco, 13. While it is generally held that legislative bodies should be larger than administrative bodies, in the United States we find a tendency to reduce the membership of city councils as their functions become more and more purely legislative. A great outcry has been raised by reformers against the unwieldy municipal assembly of 89 members provided for Greater New York in the new charter. Judge Blandin, of Cleveland, who was the principal author of that city's famous "federal charter," which provided for a council of 20 members, declared at the Minneapolis Conference in 1895 [1] that " The council is too large a body, and should be elected at large, not by districts. A council of three or five would be better than more. It is a common fault, in my opinion, that all legislative bodies from Congress down are too numerous bodies." In New York and Brooklyn the board of estimate and apportionment, which is in reality the local legislative body in matters connected with the budget, is composed of five members. In a comparison of the size of municipal councils in European and American cities, possibly it would be more just to set the European council by the side of the American commonwealth legislature, which has in many cases taken over to itself a large part of the functions of a municipal council. The legislatures of American commonwealths are generally quite large bodies. In New York there are 200 members; in Massachusetts, 280; in Rhode Island, 110; in Pennsylvania, 254; in Delaware, 30; in Georgia, 219; in Texas, 159; in Michigan, 132; in Illinois, 204; in North Da-

[1] *Proceedings*, p. 115.

kota, 93; in Colorado, 100; in Nevada, 45; in California, 120. Of the 45 commonwealths, only ten have legislatures with less than 100 members; while in eight of the commonwealths, the legislatures have a membership of 200 or more. New Hampshire has the most numerous body, the members numbering 387 in 1895.

§ 87. Organization into chambers. — The European world is practically unanimous on the side of the unicameral council. The German councils, however, are almost an exception to this rule. For in reality the executive board of magistrates has many of the characteristics of a second chamber. The analogy of the Federal Council in its relation to the Imperial Reichstag is striking. In the United States there is no certain rule. St. Louis, Philadelphia, and a good many other cities hold to the bicameral system. Boston, which now has a double council, has during the present year secured the passage of an act, which, if approved by the electors, will do away with the bicameral system. On the other hand, Greater New York on January 1, 1898, will come under its new system with a municipal assembly of two chambers. Dr. Lewis G. Janes,[1] writing in 1892, said that of the 28 American cities having a population of more than 100,000, only ten had the bicameral system; and of the 376 incorporated cities with more than 8000 inhabitants each, only 82 had a council of two

[1] *The Problem of City Government*, pp. 165, 166.

chambers. Even if there be only a single chamber, there is sometimes a differentiation in the membership. English cities have councillors and aldermen. New York used to have aldermen and assistant aldermen. Until recently about one-third of the Brooklyn aldermen were elected at large, while the rest were chosen in districts. Where there are two chambers, almost invariably one is smaller than the other and chosen for a different term and often in a different way. Sometimes the two chambers meet together for certain purposes. In Atlanta, Ga., they always meet together except for passing the budget and creating debt.[1] In Memphis, Tenn., a very peculiar organization of the municipal council is maintained. The body consists of eight persons, being the members of two boards elected by the people of the city at large, — the board of fire and police commissioners, consisting of three members, and the board of public works, consisting of five members. The body thus formed is called the legislative council. The natural tendency toward unity in municipal councils is evidenced by the common practice of appointing joint standing committees of the two chambers in those cities where the bicameral system prevails. The attempt to introduce the separation of powers into the municipal government of New York by the charter of 1830 was

[1] *Proceedings of the Baltimore Conference for Good City Government*, p. 97.

rendered abortive by the system of joint executive standing committees appointed by the two chambers of the council.[1] Joint standing committees are appointed by the councils of Philadelphia, Pittsburg, Providence, Pawtucket, Springfield, Mass., New Haven, and Lynn, and probably of about every city that has the bicameral system. Even the German cities have joint standing committees of the magistracy and the town council.

§ 88. **Methods of procedure.** — These are usually to a great extent under the control of the council itself. But it is customary in charters and general municipal acts to require publicity of the council's sessions, special majorities for the passage of certain kinds of acts, publication of proposed or enacted ordinances, and other details in the organization of the council's activity. The Greater New York charter[2] furnishes a remarkable example of laws requiring special majorities for the passage of certain measures by the council of a city. It reads thus: "Every legislative act of the municipal assembly shall be by ordinance or resolution. No ordinance or resolution shall be passed except by a vote of a majority of all the members elected to each house. In case any ordinance or resolution involves the expenditure of money, the creation of a debt, or the grant of a franchise, the votes of three-fourths of all the members elected to each house shall be necessary to its passage.

---

[1] See Durand, *op. cit.*, Chap. II.   [2] Sect. 39.

No money shall be expended for any celebration, procession, funeral ceremony, reception, or entertainment of any kind or on any occasion, unless by the votes of four-fifths of all the members elected to each house." It is then provided that no additional allowance beyond the legal claim under any contract shall be made except by the unanimous vote of each house. In the next section it is provided that ordinances and resolutions may be passed over the mayor's veto by an absolute two-thirds vote of each house; but if they involve expenditure or the granting of a franchise an absolute five-sixths vote is required for their repassage. An interesting provision of the new charter of Buffalo[1] is to the effect that "no action of the common council shall be of force unless it shall have originated in the board of aldermen and shall have been approved by the board of councilmen." Amendments may be suggested by the latter board, however. The most important feature of the council's internal organization is its committees. They are usually appointed for all of the various departments of the city's work. The list is sometimes very long. The "board of legislation" of Cincinnati has 16 standing committees; the common council of Grand Rapids, Mich., has 17; the city council of Lynn has 18 joint committees, besides eight committees of the mayor and aldermen, and three committees

[1] Laws of New York, 1891, Chap. 105.

of the common council; the common council of Rochester has 17 standing committees; the council of Toronto has nine; the councils of Philadelphia, 25; the council of Dublin, Ireland, about 15; the council of Paris had eight in 1883; the council of Manchester has 16; the board of supervisors of San Francisco, 12. The committees of most American city councils are appointed by the presiding officers. In other countries committees are chosen by the councils themselves. This is the case also in a few of our own cities, including New York, Chicago, San Francisco, and Wilmington, Del. In Grand Rapids, Mich., the mayor, who presides over the council, appoints all committees, subject to the consent of the council. If that consent is refused, the committees are elected by ballot. In most cities the council reserves to itself the right to elect a committee whenever it so decides, though appointment by the presiding officer is the rule. The committees are, under the "council system," really commissions at the head of the several departments of administration.

§ 89. **Sessions of the council.**—In France, where the idea of the council as the municipal legislature is clearest and most logically carried out, there are four regular sessions a year with their maximum duration fixed by law, though in practice frequent adjourned meetings are held. This idea of fixing the regular sessions of the council in the charter or municipal law has been adopted in a few cases for American cities. In Kansas City the regular sessions of the council are to be held on the first Monday of every month according to the terms of the law governing cities of the second class in Missouri. The laws of Maryland governing the city of Baltimore require that the council shall hold its annual meeting on a certain day in November, and continue in session for no longer than 120 days. But power is granted to the council to provide for regular sessions by ordinance. As a rule, however, the municipal council in the United States, the British Empire, and Germany meets according to its own by-laws, usually once a week.

§ 90. **The powers of the council.** — The powers given to the council may be an important factor in determining its form of organization; and on the other hand, where the forms of organization and the methods of procedure have already been fixed, they may have a good deal of influence in fixing the powers and limitations of the council. The two problems are interdependent. We may say that the extent and nature of the council's powers and duties are determined by the prevailing theory of governmental functions, the amount of home rule granted to the city, the method of central governmental control, and the system of municipal organization itself. Only an imperfect classification of the council's powers and duties is possible. A tentative outline of the main divisions, however, is presented in the following paragraphs.

§ 91. **Powers over its own organization.** — These powers of the council include the determination of the election and qualifications of its members, the election of its officers, the adoption of rules of procedure, etc. The council is generally granted a pretty full degree of liberty in these matters. The charter of Greater New York makes the action of each house of the municipal assembly subject to judicial review where members are expelled or their qualifications determined. In section 27 it is provided that "Each of said bodies [the two houses of the assembly] shall determine the rules of its own proceedings; shall each be the judge of the election returns and qualifications of its own members, subject, however, to review by *certiorari* of any court of competent jurisdiction; shall each keep a journal of its proceedings; shall each sit with open doors; shall each have the authority to compel the attendance of absent members, and to punish its members for disorderly behavior; and to expel any member with the concurrence of two-thirds of all the members elected to such body. Every member so expelled shall thereby forfeit all his rights and powers, subject, however, to judicial review on *certiorari*." The council or upper chamber of the municipal assembly of Greater New York is authorized to appoint a clerk; but his term is fixed at six years, and he can be removed only on charges subject to judicial review. Sometimes the council of a city cannot choose its presiding officer. This is the case where the mayor elected by the people presides, as in Chicago and San Francisco, and in those European countries where the mayor is an appointee of the central government. It is also true in the present New York where the "president of the board of aldermen," who is also *vice-mayor* of the city, is elected by the citizens. In Greater New York the president of the upper house of the assembly will be chosen in the same way. In some New England cities where the bicameral system is in use, the mayor presides over the upper chamber. The rules of procedure are generally more or less fixed by charter provisions, so far as they relate to the manner of voting, the publication of proposed ordinances, the delay required after the introduction of a measure before its final passage, and some such matters.

§ 92. **General legislative powers.** — The council is generally granted the power to pass local laws and enforce obedience to them by fine and imprisonment. In the United States the subjects which can be treated by municipal by-laws are usually enumerated at length.[1] It is generally held that where there is an enumeration of powers accompanied by a general grant, the latter only completes the authority of the corporation *in reference to the powers enumerated*. The charters of American cities describe the powers of the council

[1] See Goodnow, *Municipal Home Rule*, Chap. IV.

with elaborate detail. The charter of Albany, N.Y., for example, specifies the general ordinance power under 35 heads; in the general Municipal Incorporations Act of Illinois the powers of the council are enumerated under 96 heads; the general law of Pennsylvania enumerates 46 purposes for which cities of the second, third, and fourth classes may enact ordinances. The system of enumerated powers has a foothold in Canada also. The Ontario Municipal Act, under section 479, enumerates 36 purposes for which by-laws may be passed. Other purposes are more extensively described in other sections. In England the municipal councils are given a general ordinance power, but other powers are enumerated, chiefly in a long list of acts referring to special branches of administration. An interesting attempt to make an enumeration of powers that shall not be exclusive is found in the Greater New York charter. Section 49 describes the general ordinance power of the municipal assembly in 31 subsections. Section 50 then provides that "The foregoing or other enumeration of powers in this act shall not be held to limit the legislative power of the municipal assembly, which, in addition thereto, may exercise all of the powers vested in the city of New York by this act or otherwise." This provision, however, seems to confer upon the municipal assembly all of the powers — subject to specific limitations — *that have been granted to the city by express provisions of law.* In Europe a general grant is made to the local councils. Professor Goodnow says:[1] "The student of American municipal corporations is at once struck, upon his perusal of these continental municipal corporations acts, with the complete absence of any enumeration of municipal powers; and until he understands the meaning of the phrase, 'the council shall govern by its decisions the affairs of the city,' he is apt to believe on account of the many instances where central approval of some sort is required in order that the action of municipal corporations may be valid, that the sphere of free action of the continental municipal corporation is a very narrow one. But so soon as he understands that this phrase means that the presumption is always in favor of the competence of municipal corporations, and that the central administration has power relative to municipal corporations only where such power has been expressly granted, he perceives that the system adopted for permitting municipal corporations to participate in the work of government is exactly the reverse of that which is adopted in the American and the original English system; and that unless the central administrative control is very great, the continental corporations have really under it greater local powers than are possessed by American municipal corporations. While our method is one of

[1] *Municipal Problems*, pp. 252-254.

enumerated powers, the continental method is one of general grant of power, subject to specific enumerated restrictions. The municipal corporation may do anything where power has not been conferred specifically upon some other authority, and is subjected to a central control only where the law specifically and expressly provides for such a control." The most important of the strictly legislative powers granted to the council is the power to tax and to borrow money to be paid out of the taxes later on. As the power to tax is the vital power of sovereignty, it is everywhere recognized that city councils must be kept at least theoretically under a strict control in their budgetary legislation. In New York city the budget, in so far as it is determined by local authorities, is fixed by the board of estimate and apportionment, which is composed of five *ex officio* members: the mayor, the comptroller, and the president of the board of aldermen, all elected, and the corporation counsel and the president of the department of taxes and assessments, appointed by the mayor.

§ 93. **Corporate powers.** — We may distinguish under this heading those powers of the council which, though legislative in character, correspond more to the ordinary local and special legislation of the central legislature. The determination of policy and the formulation of particular projects for public works and local improvements are included here. The distinction between "general legislative powers" and "corporate powers," as the terms are here used, is seen in the English system, where the former are included in a general grant contained in the provisions of the municipal code, while the latter are usually provided for by special and local legislation or by the municipal "clauses acts." In the exercise of its "corporate powers" a city council acts more as the governing body of a corporation; while in the exercise of its "general legislative powers" the council acts more as a local branch of the general government.

§ 94. **Powers of direct administration.** — These are of great importance where the "council system" prevails. Committees and individual members of the council are given powers and duties in the direct carrying out of laws and projects. This is the case in England, and perhaps to a limited extent in Germany. Up to the middle of this century the aldermen and the assistant aldermen of New York city were given certain important administrative powers in their respective wards, particularly over the management and care of the streets.

§ 95. **Judicial powers.** — Formerly the municipal council was more of a court than anything else. The first council of New York, established in 1652, was almost exclusively a judicial body.[1] In Philadelphia the aldermen were given important

---

[1] See Durand, *op. cit.*, Chap. I.; and Mary L. Booth, *History of New York City*, p. 136.

judicial functions by Penn's charter, granted in 1701. An act of 1796 took away their legislative powers, and they remained judicial officers only, and were henceforth, until 1854, appointed by the governor of the commonwealth.[1] By the act of 1854 the aldermen became elective, two being chosen in each ward. They were supplanted by magistrates under the constitution of 1873. In other American cities the aldermen usually sat in the mayor's or recorder's court, and had the powers of justices of the peace up to about the middle of this century. The judicial powers of the council as a body have, however, been reduced to a minimum, and are everywhere of little importance.

§ 96. **Powers of control over municipal officers.** — In almost every system of public law, and especially in countries where the democratic principle has gained a foothold, the legislative body, whether of the state or of the municipality, is given a large measure of control over the executive and administrative officers of government. Where the administration is centralized, the legislative control is exercised directly over the principal administrative officers only. The legislative control over the administration is justified on the grounds that law-making is the fundamental power of government, that the legislature or the city

[1] See Allinson and Penrose, *Philadelphia*, pp. 14, 49, 61, 62, 65, 66, 160.

council is a deliberative body, and that it is made up of direct representatives of the people, whose mandates are frequently renewed. In cities the control of the council over the municipal administration is enforced in many ways. Sometimes the council has the power to organize the departments according to its own ideas of right and expediency. Sometimes the council can appoint city officers and remove them at pleasure, or for some specified cause. Usually the right of examining officials and investigating the work of departments is given to the council. Reports are made to the council of the work done in the several municipal departments, or may be called for by that body. But the most important of all the levers which the council may use to influence administration is its financial power. The taxes are levied, the franchises sold, and the appropriations made by order of the municipal legislative body. Intelligence and tact usually control in government. And so the importance of the control exercised by the council in any particular city depends upon the wisdom and strength of its members, as well as of the administrative officers at the head of the departments.

§ 97. **Duties, limitations, emoluments, etc., of councilmen.** — The duties of the council are in connection with those acts in which the council is regarded as the agent of the central government for the enforcement of law and the fulfilment of obligations. In France and Germany the authorities of the central administration have the power to insert items of the so-called "obligatory expenditures" in the municipal budgets, where these have been omitted by the councils. In the United States many of the items of a city's budget are dictated by the state legislature or by the courts in the enforcement of obligations imposed upon the city by the legislature. The special limitations upon the council, like the disqualifications for suffrage or office holding, are negative and exceptional in their character, though numerous and important. They refer generally to procedure and the personal interests of the councillors. Usually members of the council are forbidden to be interested directly or indirectly in any public contracts with the city, or in the purchase of the city's real estate, or in the sale of supplies to the city. Sometimes a councillor is declared to be ineligible, during the term for which he was elected, to any office which may have been created, or whose emoluments may have been increased by the council during that time. The limitations upon the council's procedure have been referred to. There are often direct limitations also upon the powers of the council, as when it is forbidden to contract debt without special authorization, or to expend money for entertainments and celebrations. The emoluments of membership in the council vary according to the importance of that body and the dignity of each particular city. Generally no salaries or very small ones are attached to the position of councillors. In Greater New York the president of the council will receive a salary of $5000 a year; other members of the council will get $1500; and members of the board of aldermen will get $1000. In Cincinnati each member of the board of legislation gets $10 for every session of the board at which he is present from beginning to end. In Grand Rapids, Mich., the salary of an alderman is $350 a year. In Wilmington, Del., each member of the council receives $1 for every council meeting he attends, and 50 cents for every committee meeting he attends, his total compensation in any one month not to exceed $20. By the new charter of New Orleans, "The members of the council shall receive $20 each for attendance at each regular monthly meeting of said body, provided that such members shall have attended all called or special meetings held during such month."[1] The English Municipal Corporations Act of 1835[2] provided that elected officers, except the mayor, should accept office under penalty of a fine not exceeding £50 for refusal or neglect to serve. The mayor-elect could be fined £100 for refusal. The exact amount of the fines was to be fixed in each city by a by-law. Under the present municipal code the fines for non-acceptance of office are to be reckoned at half the above sums, if there is no by-law

[1] Sect. 10. [2] Sect. 51.

fixing their amounts. By Baron Stein's *City Ordinance* of 1808 compulsory service in the council and on the municipal boards was made the rule in Prussia. At that time even voting was compulsory, and repeated failures to exercise the franchise might be punished by the withdrawal of the right. In Prussia, France, and England the council members are unsalaried. As the Prussian city councillors are unpaid, the principle of obligatory service is so far relaxed that a councillor may withdraw from office after having served at least three years of the six for which he was elected. In both Prussia and England there are provisions made for the exemption from the obligation of official service of persons who are above a certain age, or who have served within a certain number of years, or who are entitled in some other way to special consideration. Compulsory service was the policy of a good many early American charters. This was the case in the Dongan and Montgomerie charters of New York (1686 and 1730); in the Dongan charter of Albany (1686); in the Detroit charter of 1824; in the Buffalo charter of 1832; in the Rochester charter of 1834.

IV. *The Head of the Corporation*

§ 98. The mayor or head of the corporation. — With the application of the theory of the separation of powers to municipal government the importance of the executive head is greatly increased. In fact, recent American city charters make the mayor the most important part of the municipal government. His relative importance is greatly increased by the practice of the state legislature in assuming local legislative functions, thus leaving the city council a body of little power in many cases. We hear a good deal of the "municipal dictator" in discussions of the recent tendencies of charter-making for American cities. In Greater New York the mayor elected for a term of four years will have the absolute power of appointment so far as the heads of the administrative departments, except those of finance and education, are concerned, and for the first six months of his term will have an unlimited power of removal. With a strongly fortified veto power over the acts of the municipal assembly and very great powers as a member of the board of estimate and apportionment, the sinking fund commission, and the board of public improvements, the mayor of New York will certainly be an official of great importance. The *maires* of French cities, the *bürgermeisters* of German towns, and the heads of municipalities in continental Europe generally, are officers of nearly as much importance and power as the American mayor. The importance of the French mayor arises from the fact that he is vested with the whole administrative function of the city, and is the representative of the central government as well. The German burgomaster gets his importance from his professional character and his long term of office, which is usually twelve years or for life. The English mayor is chiefly a spectacular and honorary functionary as far as legal powers are concerned. Being elected every year by the council, he is in no way the representative of the popular will, as an American mayor is; he does not represent the central government or control the municipal administration as a French mayor does; and he has no long term of office, as the German burgomaster has. The English mayor has no veto power, and no administrative or executive power save as a member of the council. He is, however, a justice of the peace and represents the dignity of the corporation. Usually also as an experienced councillor and a distinguished citizen he has great influence in the city government.

§ 99. **How the mayor is chosen.** — We may consider several points in regard to the position, powers, and duties of the head of the corporation. First, of course, is the question of how the mayor is chosen. In the United States and Canada the mayor is elected by the people. But there are exceptions to this rule. The city of Memphis, Tenn., has a peculiar system of government, the result of local financial troubles into which the city fell some twenty years ago. A board of three fire and police commissioners, elected by the people, chooses its own president; and he is *ex-*

officio mayor of the city. The mayors of cities in the state of New York were appointed by the governor in council till 1821, and then were elected by the municipal councils until about 1840. It seems, also, that the rule of the mayor's election by the people does not hold throughout Canada. The city of Quebec, as also the city of Montreal, has followed the English system pretty closely. The council of Quebec is composed of thirty members, three being elected every second year from each of the ten quarters of the city. This council elects the mayor from its own membership for a term of two years. In Great Britain, the Australian Colonies, and the countries of continental Europe the mayor is elected by the council, or in some cases appointed by the central government. The latter is true in Belgium, Holland, Denmark, and the smaller communes of Italy; and also in Sweden, and possibly some other European countries.[1] The approval of the central government is required for the appointment of the German burgomasters[2] and the four chief executives of the city of Copenhagen.[3]

§ 100. **The mayor's term of service.** — In the United States mayors are selected for terms ranging from one to five years. In most New England

---

[1] See Shaw, *Municipal Government in Continental Europe*, pp. 225, 238, and 253; Ferron, *op. cit.*, pp. 230, 231, and 234.

[2] Goodnow, *Comparative Administrative Law*, Vol. I., p. 333.

[3] Ferron, *op. cit.*, p. 231.

cities, including Cambridge, Portland, Providence, Worcester, Springfield, and New Bedford, the mayor is elected for a single year. This was the case in Boston also until 1895. The term is two years in a great many cities, including Detroit, San Francisco, Brooklyn, Newark, Baltimore, Chicago, Cleveland, Omaha, Minneapolis, Milwaukee, Indianapolis, Richmond, Salt Lake City, Seattle, Atlanta, New Haven, Boston, Wilmington, Del., and Bridgeport. Allegheny, Reading, and Scranton, in Pennsylvania, have mayors elected for three years. The term of office is four years in Greater New York, Buffalo, Philadelphia, Louisville, St. Louis, and New Orleans. The mayor of Jersey City is elected for a term of five years. The mayor of Atlanta is not eligible to reëlection for a succeeding term. This will be true also of the mayor of Greater New York. By the first city charter of New Haven, granted in 1784, the mayor was elected by the people, but held office during the pleasure of the General Assembly of the commonwealth. This provision lasted until 1826; and during those forty-two years the city had only four mayors, two of whom died in office.[1] The mayors of Hartford also were, until 1825, elected by the freemen, and held office during the pleasure of the General Assembly.[2] In England the mayor is

[1] See Levermore, *Town and City Government of New Haven*, Johns Hopkins University Studies, 4th series, p. 453.
[2] See *Municipal Register* of Hartford, 1896, p. 4.

chosen annually. The mayor's term in France is four years, and in Germany, where he is a trained and professional officer, his term is usually twelve years or for life.

§ 101. **Official position and responsibility of the mayor.** — In all cases the mayor is the representative head of the city corporation. In France, Belgium, and Italy he is also the local representative of the central government.[1] In many cases the central government may remove the mayor, either arbitrarily, as in France,[2] or for cause, as in some of the American commonwealths.[3] The governor may remove mayors for cause in Michigan. A similar power is delegated to the governor of New York by the charters of New York city and several other cities of that state.

§ 102. **Legislative powers of the mayor.** — The powers of the mayor as a member and president of the council have in the United States generally been superseded by the veto power which he exercises over the legislative acts of the council. In almost all cases the mayor no longer has a vote as a member of the council in American cities, except a casting vote in those cities where he is still the presiding officer at the council's meetings. Almost everywhere also, at least in the important

---

[1] Goodnow, *op. cit.*, Vol. I., p. 288; Shaw, *op. cit.*, pp. 176, 225, 256.

[2] French Municipal Code, Art. 86.

[3] See *ante*, pp. 105–107.

cities, the mayor has the veto power over the acts of the council. In many of the more recent charters the mayor is given the power to disapprove parts of measures, such as particular items in the appropriation bills. This is an extremely important addition to the veto power as it is vested in the President in the national constitution. The present charter of Albany, for instance, provides that "The mayor may object to one or more and to each of the items of the annual budget . . . or may reduce the amount thereof, while approving of the other portions of the budget." In this case it requires a four-fifths vote of all the members elected to the council to override the mayor's veto. In most cases city ordinances take effect without the mayor's signature, unless he returns them to the council within a certain number of days. But in the new charter of New Orleans the failure of the mayor to approve an ordinance, or to return it to the council with his veto within five days or at the next session, has the same effect as a veto. In most cities the veto power is not absolute, but requires a two-thirds vote of the council to overcome it. In Bridgeport, Conn., the mayor has only a suspensive veto, the repassage of ordinances in the face of his objections requiring only an ordinary majority vote. The "act for the government of cities of the second class," passed by the New York legislature of 1897, but vetoed by Governor Black, provided that the mayor's veto could be overridden only by an absolute three-fourths vote of the members of the council. The suspensive veto of the mayors in the cities of the state of New York over special city legislation passed by the state legislature should not go unmentioned.[1] In the German system of municipal government the burgomaster and his executive staff have pretty complete control of city legislation. They initiate measures, to which the council gives its assent; and then they elaborate and carry to execution the projects or regulations determined upon. The powers of the Prussian town executive in municipal legislation have already been referred to on a previous page.[2] The power of the executive in the initiation of measures seems to be more a matter of practice than of legal theory. The executive, however, has a legal veto power over the resolutions of the council. This veto power is absolute, pending an appeal to the supervising authorities. The veto is exercised chiefly for the purpose of keeping the council within its lawful jurisdiction.[3] The French mayor has to prepare the budget and lay it before the council.[4] In New York city the mayor possesses extensive power as a member of the board of estimate and apportion-

---

[1] See Goodnow, *Municipal Home Rule*, pp. 96–98, and *ante*, pp. 88, 89.

[2] See *ante*, pp. 144–146.

[3] See Goodnow, *Municipal Problems*, p. 98.

[4] French Municipal Code, Arts. 90 and 95.

ment which practically exercises the whole power of the corporation in levying taxes and making appropriations. The mayor will preside over this board in Greater New York. The board will consist of five members, two of whom are to be appointees of the mayor. The municipal assembly will have power to reduce or strike out particular items in the appropriations, subject to the mayor's veto. And it will require a five-sixths vote of both houses to override his veto on these matters. It should be noted also that the mayor of Greater New York will have much legislative power, in an indirect way through the board of public improvements, of which he is a member, and of which he appoints eight of the ten other members. This board prepares all ordinances relating to the waterworks, the regulation, cleaning, maintenance, and use of the streets, the construction and repair of public markets, the laying of pipes, wires, and tubes underground, public lighting, the erection and repair of public buildings (except those pertaining to certain specified departments), the rates of fare on bridges, and the making of all contracts for public work and supplies. These ordinances must be enacted or rejected by the municipal assembly without amendment.[1] The mayor also appoints the boards at the head of the health, police, park, and buildings departments, and the head of the fire department, all of which have more or less

[1] See Charter of Greater New York, sects. 47, 416, 417.

independent ordinance power.[1] The school boards of the several boroughs are appointed by the mayor, and the general board of education is made up of delegates from these boards. All of these bodies have extensive ordinance power.[2]

§ 103. **The mayor's judicial powers.** — The mayor is almost everywhere a magistrate *ex officio*. The English mayor is a justice of the peace during his term of office and for one year thereafter. Originally in the United States the mayor was the chief judge of the mayor's court. The recorder, who was at first both judge and member of the council, at a later period lost his seat in that body and became a professional judicial officer. The mayor's court in some cases came to be called the recorder's court, and the recorder in the long run supplanted the mayor in most of his important judicial functions. Before the middle of the present century, American mayors were commonly judges of the city court. But at the present time the mayor's judicial functions in this and other countries have been for the most part transferred to the regular judicial officers.

§ 104. **The mayor's administrative powers.** — In Geneva and the cities of France the mayor is given full charge of the municipal administration.[3]

---

[1] See Charter of Greater New York, sects. 47, 272, 300, 610, 645, 739, and 1172.

[2] *Ibid.*, sects. 1061, 1062, 1070, and 1090.

[3] Ferron, *op. cit.*, p. 228; French Municipal Code, Art. 82.

Officers are appointed and removed by him, and even his deputies elected by the council have no powers or duties except as he makes delegations and assignments to them. In the United States, also, the administrative powers of the mayor have been greatly increased in recent years by the grant to him of the powers to appoint and to remove city officers. His direct administrative powers are, however, usually not extensive in this country, except where he is the head of the police department. Although the mayor has lost most of his old judicial functions, he is everywhere recognized as a peace officer. As such he is charged with the suppression of riots and the maintenance of order. As the head of the city government he may develop into a military officer when there is need in much the same way that the governors of the commonwealths and the President of the United States do. In some cities this position of the mayor is logically maintained by his investiture with the immediate management of the police force. In Buffalo the mayor is a member of the police board, but does not have to take an active part in the administration of the department so long as the two other police commissioners agree. In Cincinnati and St. Louis the mayor is *ex officio* a member of the police board, the other members being appointed by the governor. The mayors of Chicago and Minneapolis are themselves vested with the direct management of the police.

In Germany the burgomaster's administrative powers are very great, though not exclusive as in France.

§ 105. Privileges and emoluments of the mayoralty. — Under the English system of municipal government the mayor's position entitles him to the first place of honor in the city, and entails upon him in many cases, it is said, a large expenditure of money. The dignity of the municipality must be maintained by dinners and receptions at which the mayor officiates. Although English municipal councillors are not salaried, the council is authorized to appropriate money for the mayor's salary to reimburse him for his expenses as head of the corporation. The statement is somewhere made that in one of the cities of England the council is in the habit of voting to the mayor as salary, sums to be expended on certain projects for which the council has no right to make any direct appropriation under the law. This is a convenient scheme for using the mayor's position to evade the limitations imposed on the city by the system of enumerated powers. In France the mayors are, immediately after their election, made the guests of the authorities of the department in which their respective communes are situated. In this way the representatives of the central government seek to win over at the outset the locally chosen executives to the interests of the national administration. The pomp and display connected with their first introduction to the central authorities are said to be very effective in making the mayors of French communes loyal to the supervisory authority of the government at Paris. The municipal executives in France are unpaid, but in Germany they receive regular salaries. In the United States the salaries of mayors are sometimes very large. The mayor of Greater New York will receive $15,000 a year. The mayor of the present New York gets $10,000; the mayor of Philadelphia, $12,000; of Boston, $10,000; of Baltimore, $5000; of Chicago, $7000; of Minneapolis, $2000; of St. Louis, $5000; of New Orleans, $6000; of Denver, $5000; of San Francisco, $4200; of Pittsburg, $7000.

V. *The Administrative Departments*

§ 106. Separation of executive and administrative functions. — It is specially convenient in treating of city government to separate the executive and the administrative authorities. When the system of separation of powers began to be introduced into American cities in imitation of the national and state governments, the ununified administrative system of the states was more generally followed than the centralized, unified system of the national administration. Although the general form of government in the commonwealths is similar to the form of the federal government, the administrative systems are quite different. In the national system the

President through his power of appointment and removal has come to be the almost autocratic head of a centralized administration. But in the commonwealths the governors' powers of appointment and removal are generally very limited. Many state officers are elected by the people, and most of the local administrative functions of the government are performed by locally chosen officers. Thus the governor of an American commonwealth is an executive officer, but only to a limited extent an administrative officer. The centralization of administrative responsibility in the mayor's office by recent city charters is in imitation of our national system. The division of the administrative responsibility among independent city departments and boards is in imitation of the commonwealth system. When the mayor was first made an independent authority in our cities, he became the executive but not the administrative head of the city government. Administration, at first under the control of council committees, came to be parcelled out to various boards or officers independent of each other and subject only to legislative and judicial control. This peculiarly American fact, together with the more general fact that administration pure and simple is far more important relatively in municipal than in national government, makes the separation of the administrative from the executive authorities in the outline here presented quite natural and practicable.

§ 107. **The administrative departments.** — It is in the organization of the departments of municipal administration that the greatest variety is found in the practice of cities. The investigator who has concluded that a respectable classification of municipal functions is impossible, must certainly recoil before the task of classifying the details of municipal administrative organization. Each city has built up its local machinery by small increments from the beginning of its corporate life until the present time. Perhaps comparisons are more odious in this field than in any other, at least for any one with a passion for logical arrangement. Only a few topics, important in the study of administrative organization, can be mentioned here.

§ 108. **Number of the departments and their spheres of activity.** — In some cases practically the whole administration is divided into three or four great departments. In Pittsburg, for example, there are the three departments of public safety, public works, and public charities. It should be said, however, that a good deal of the city administration is not included in these three departments. There are, also, a board of education, a city attorney, a board of assessors, a treasurer, a delinquent tax collector, a controller, and a city clerk. But the department of public safety in Pittsburg, as in Philadelphia, Allegheny, and most European cities, includes the police, fire, and health services,

o

and building inspection. In Indianapolis the health administration is not included in the department of public safety, but is combined with the public charities administration. The city of Brooklyn has fifteen full-fledged departments, as follows: finance, audit, treasury, collection, arrears, law, assessment, police, health, fire, buildings, city works, parks, public instruction, and charities and correction. The Greater New York charter provides for eighteen departments, as follows: finance; taxes and assessments; law; police; health; fire; buildings; highways; water supply; bridges; street cleaning; sewers; public buildings, lighting, and supplies; parks; docks, slips and ferries; education; charities; and correction. Boston has perhaps lagged farther behind than other great American cities in the consolidation of her administrative departments. She has at the present time some thirty-three separate executive departments, whose heads are appointed by the mayor, subject to confirmation by the aldermen. These are: (1) the board of assessors; (2) the board of fire commissioners; (3) the board of health; (4) the Boston city hospital; (5) the board of trustees of public library; (6) trustees of Mt. Hope cemetery; (7) the board of park commissioners; (8) the board of commissioners of public institutions; (9) the board of registrars of voters; (10) overseers of the poor in the city of Boston; (11) board of commissioners of sinking funds; (12)

Boston water board; (13) city architect; (14) city auditor; (15) city collector; (16) city engineer; (17) superintendent of ferries; (18) superintendent of public buildings; (19) inspector of milk and vinegar; (20) inspector of provisions; (21) superintendent of lamps; (22) superintendent of markets; (23) superintendent of printing; (24) inspector of buildings; (25) superintendent of public grounds; (26) city registrar; (27) sealer of weights and measures; (28) superintendent of streets; (29) city surveyor; (30) city treasurer; (31) water registrar; (32) commissioner of wires; (33) corporation counsel and city solicitor. Besides these there are the board of street commissioners, the school committee, and the county officers, elected by the people, and the police board, appointed by the governor.[1] It is evident that the traditions of the New England town, with its almost numberless officials, are still strong in Boston. In American cities there is a tendency to create a very comprehensive department of public works and public improvements. Six departments of the Greater New York are to be united under a supervisory board of public improvements. This scheme was copied directly from St. Louis. The department of public works in Cleveland, Indianapolis, Pittsburg, Philadelphia, and Buffalo covers almost as extensive a field of municipal functions. In Manchester, England, the council is divided up

[1] See Matthews, *op. cit.*, Chap. I.

into sixteen great standing committees, most of which are at the head of separate departments of administration.[1] In Paris, police, fire service, and the protection of public health are united under the prefect of police. What functions shall be united in one department, and what functions shall be distributed among several departments, are questions to which the municipal institutions of the world give no coherent answer.

§ 109. **Relations of the departments to each other and to the central authority of the corporation.** — As has been indicated, many American cities have scarcely provided for any mutual or unifying relations between the departments. The city of Cleveland has, however, established the cabinet system, which requires the heads of departments to meet together under the mayor's presidency at frequent intervals for the discussion of municipal policies.[2] The boards of estimate and appointment in New York city and Brooklyn partially accomplish the same end by a different means. These boards certainly introduce a much-desired unity into the financial policies of the two cities; and as all of the departments are dependent upon these boards to a very large extent for the means of carrying on their functions, the power of the boards in controlling departmental

---

[1] See Shaw, *Municipal Government in Great Britain*, pp. 149, 150.

[2] Wilcox, *op. cit.*, p. 149.

policies is greatly enlarged. Another important means of unifying the policy of the departments in Greater New York will be the board of public improvements to which reference has already been made. In Cincinnati a large number of the city administrative functions are put under the direct management of the "board of administration," which consists of four members appointed by the mayor equally from the two leading political parties. Under the "administrative system" introduced into the government of New Orleans in 1870, the mayor and administrators usually met as such and gave public hearings before their regular meetings as the municipal council. By the present charter of New Orleans the mayor is required "to call together the executive officers and heads of departments for consultation and advice upon the affairs of the city at least once a month." The unity of the administration is in most cities, of course, attained through the control of the mayor or of the council, if attained at all. The best way to bring about unity of administration through the control of the mayor is to require him to call the department officers together for consultation at frequent intervals and to give him full powers of appointment and removal over them. The system which provides a mayor and adjuncts in France, and a burgomaster and staff in Germany and other European countries, effects the result in a seemingly satisfactory manner.

The same may be said of the English council system.

§ 110. The organization of heads of departments. Appointment. — The main points in regard to the heads of departments to be considered are: the source of appointment, the tenure and term of office, and the nature of the head as being a commission or a single officer. Appointments are usually made by the mayor, by the council, or by both. In France the mayor has full appointing power. In England and Prussia it is the council that appoints the heads of departments. In the United States about every conceivable method has been tried. In the early days of council government the city officials were generally chosen by the council. After that the plan of election by the people was tried. And in these days of "model charters" the mayor's power of appointment has been greatly increased. There are cases also of the appointment of municipal boards by the governor of the state or their election by the state legislature. The old system of appointment by the council still continues in some cities, especially the smaller ones. In Pawtucket, R.I., for example, the city council elects annually a city treasurer, a judge of probate, a city solicitor, a city auditor, a collector of taxes, and a number of commissioners of highways and overseers of the poor. In Minneapolis and Salt Lake City, also, the council has the appointment of a large number of important city officers. The upper house of the municipal assembly of New York will have the appointment of the city clerk, whose salary is to be $7000 a year. The best example of the election of a municipal board by the state legislature that has come to the attention of the writer, is the choice of the Baltimore police board by the general assembly of Maryland in joint session. At one time the members of the board of metropolitan police in New York were elected by the legislature.[1] It has very often happened that the first members of a municipal board or commission have been named by the legislatures of the states. There are many instances of the policy by which municipal boards are appointed by the governor of the commonwealth. In St. Louis there are three boards appointed in this way, there are two in Baltimore, at least three in San Francisco, two in Denver, and one or more in at least all of the following cities: Omaha, Cincinnati, Toledo, New Orleans, Wilmington, Boston, and Detroit. The members of the police board and of the park board in Wilmington, Del., were at first appointed by act of the legislature, but are now appointed by the associate judge of the superior court residing in New Castle county. In some cases, notably in that of New York city, where the governor once had a considerable power of

[1] Laws of New York, 1864, Chap. 41.

appointment of municipal boards, that power has been recommitted to local authorities. Probably the most common method of appointing municipal department heads in American cities is nomination by the mayor and approval by the council. In cases where this method prevails there is opportunity for a deadlock. Such a thing occurred in Baltimore in 1896, after the election of a reform mayor.[1] The size of the vote in the council required for confirmation of the mayor's nominees is an important factor in the problem. Sometimes a simple majority of the members present is required, sometimes a majority of all the members elected, and sometimes more than a simple majority of all. At the Pennsylvania legislative session of 1897, a bill was passed requiring a three-fifths vote of the select council in Philadelphia in order to confirm the mayor's nominations. The charter of Albany provides that appointments by the mayor must be considered by the council at the meeting at which they are presented, and unless rejected at that meeting or the next regular one by a majority of all the members elected, the appointments shall stand confirmed. The system of electing department officers by direct vote of the people was inaugurated in New York city by the charter of 1849,[2]

---

[1] Howard, "The Recent Revolt in Baltimore," *Proceedings of the Baltimore Conference for Good City Government*, p. 85.
[2] Sect. 20.

but soon became discredited and was abandoned in 1857.[1] The plan is still applied very generally in the case of the comptroller, the auditor or the treasurer of a city, and often also in the case of school boards, boards of public works, water commissioners, etc.

§ 111. **Term of service of department heads.** — In the United States the term of office is usually fixed at from one to eight years, subject to removal for cause or in some cases at the discretion of the appointing authority. The members of municipal boards usually hold for comparatively long terms and do not all retire at once. But in New York city even the single officers at the head of departments have in most cases a term of six years. Sometimes, as in the charters of Brooklyn and Cleveland, we find the terms of the department chiefs the same as the term of the appointing authority. In other cases the terms of the appointing and the appointed authorities differ. In Greater New York the mayor will be elected for four years, but most of his appointees will hold for two years longer unless removed by an incoming mayor during the first six months of his incumbency. The council, elected for four years, will choose a clerk for a term of six years who can be removed only for cause. In England, where the departmental administration is professional rather than political, the heads of departments

[1] Charter of 1857, sect. 19.

acting under the committees of the council generally have a permanent tenure. In France the adjuncts of the mayor and in Germany the staff officers of the burgomaster who correspond pretty closely to the heads of departments in American cities, are elected by the council for a definite term of years, but are often reëlected.

§ 112. **Nature of department heads. Boards and single commissioners.** — In Germany the head of each department is a board or commission in fact, if not in name. The same is true in the English cities, where committees of the council are the real heads of departments. The tendency in America at the present time is toward the plan of single heads. There is, however, some attempt to distinguish between departments according to the nature of their functions, some demanding a greater amount of deliberation and others more executive efficiency. In the Greater New York charter, for example, it is provided that the heads of eight of the eighteen departments shall be boards or commissions. These departments have charge of police, parks, buildings, public charities, docks and ferries, taxes and assessments, education, and health, respectively. It was thought that in each of these departments deliberation and consultation were of primary importance. The charter commission has been severely criticised for not putting the police department under a single commissioner. The departments which are to be under single commissioners are those having charge of finance, law, correction, and fire and the six which are grouped together under the general supervision of the board of public improvements. It may be said that practically everywhere the department of education is under the supervision of a board. In Cleveland, however, the school government parallels the general city government, the administrative functions being entrusted to a single school director, while the legislative functions are in the hands of a school council of seven members. The system in Buffalo is also peculiar. There the city council acts as the school board, while the administrative functions are entrusted to a popularly elected superintendent of education. We have also developed in this country the system of non-partisan or bi-partisan boards, the immediate outcome of the prevalence of the political spoils system in city government. The dominance of national political parties in municipal as well as in commonwealth governments led to the exploitation of the cities for partisan purposes. Often the political majority in a commonwealth legislature found one or more of the cities within its jurisdiction controlled by a hostile political party. In order to divide the municipal spoils, protect itself against its enemy, and make a show of non-partisan government in the cities, the party in power in the state legislature often enacted that certain departments of the administration in particular cities should be governed by boards in which more than one political party should be represented, or perhaps the two leading parties be equally represented. The "bi-partisan system," as it is called, is sometimes carried to a point where it becomes quite amusing. In Bridgeport, Conn., the common council consists of twenty members, no more than ten of whom can be elected from one political party. The five selectmen of the town, the seven sheriffs, and the two public weighers are to be elected by a system of minority representation. There are besides the following bi-partisan administrative boards, on most of which the two leading political parties must be equally represented: board of fire commissioners, board of park commissioners, board of sinking fund commissioners, board of assessors, board of relief, board of police commissioners, board of public works, board of charities, board of appraisal of benefits and damages, and board of apportionment and taxation. Practically the plan of giving the two parties equal representation on municipal boards does not seem to give non-partisan government, but rather to dissipate responsibility and induce the two parties represented to make a pool for the division of the spoils. The inefficiency of the plan even where the appointing power wishes to establish non-partisan government has been clearly illustrated by the recent long-continued deadlock in the New York police board under the presidency of Mr. Roosevelt. The best variety of the bi-partisan system is probably that which is in vogue in Buffalo. There are three such boards in that city to look after the police, fire, and public works departments, respectively. In all three cases there are two members appointed by the mayor, and they must belong to different political parties. The mayor himself is the third member of the police and fire boards, while for the board of public works a third member is chosen directly by the people. This plan, it will be seen, insures the control of the boards by the party which received the majority of the suffrages at the preceding mayoralty election; while the other party always has one member on each board. The bi-partisan system is in operation in a great many American cities, of which Cincinnati and Denver are good examples. In Michigan a law requiring appointments to be made equally from the two principal parties has been declared unconstitutional, as establishing a "test" for office in contravention to the fundamental law of the commonwealth.[1] A similar decision was handed down in 1896 by the Court of Appeals of New York in the case of *Rathbone* vs. *Wirth*,[2] which involved the constitutionality of the "Albany police bill." This act was declared void, but in this case bi-partisanship

---

[1] See the case of *Attorney General* vs. *Board of Councilmen of the City of Detroit*, 58 Mich. 213.

[2] 150 N. Y. 459.

and legislative interference were so aggravated and complex that it would be hard to make safe deductions from the court's decision.

§ 113. The organization of the subordinate departmental service. — In our detailed American charters provision is often made for the internal organization of the departments. This is, perhaps, especially true of the cities of New York state. But sometimes the council is left to organize the departments and sometimes the department chiefs themselves are given full power to organize the subordinate service. In the charters of New York city, although most of the important points in the departmental organization have been definitely set forth, it has been customary to leave the details in the hands of the heads of departments, subject of course to the financial limitations imposed by the budget. At the present time, for example, the chamberlain, who is at the head of the bureau of the treasury, receives a salary of $25,000 out of which he must pay all of the clerks and assistants that his duties may compel him to hire. The heads of departments generally in New York appoint their subordinates, divide the city into administrative districts, and proceed with their work quite independently. It should be said, however, that the internal organization of such departments as those of police, fire, and street cleaning is fixed in a great deal of detail by the charter itself. The prevalence of the spoils system and the evils resulting from it when left unchecked have led to the introduction of permanent tenure in the police and fire departments generally, and of competitive examinations for positions in all departments in a few cities of this country. General systems of competitive examinations for the civil service are in force throughout the states of New York and Massachusetts. Chicago recently adopted the optional civil service law passed by the Illinois legislature. "Civil service reform" has been adopted in Milwaukee and New Orleans also. The bill "To provide for the government of cities of over 50,000 inhabitants" introduced at the last session of the Minnesota legislature embodied a system of competitive examinations and probationary appointments. The new charter for San Francisco, which was rejected by the people in 1896, also embodied the civil service reform principle. The civil service commission was to be appointed by the mayor, and consist of three persons known by him to be devoted to the principles of civil service reform, and opposed to the system of rewarding political party service by political appointment.[1] In Chicago the present

---

[1] Proposed Charter, Art. XII., sect. 2. Section 1 of the same article was as follows: "It is hereby declared to be the intent and purpose of this charter that the government of the city and county of San Francisco and each and every department thereof shall be managed and conducted on business principles. The salaries and compensation of its clerks and employees shall be fixed and regulated from time to time, at no higher rates than those paid for the rendition of similar services in commercial employments in said city

mayor was elected on a platform protesting against the methods of enforcement of the civil service law heretofore employed in that city.[1] In the state of New York, also, an important check has been given to the progress of the principle of appointment on account of merit as determined by open competitive examinations. Governor Black's now famous civil service law was enacted at the legislative session of 1897. It provides that appointments shall be based on merit and fitness. The examinations for determining merit are to be open and competitive, and under the control of the civil service commissions. But the maximum percentage that an applicant may receive for merit is fifty. Another examination for *fitness* is to be given by the appointing authority. The maximum possible marking on this examination is also fifty per cent. The percentages received by applicants at the two examinations are to be added, and the person re-

---

or county. There shall be no discharge or removal of such clerks or employees in any of the departments of the city and county government, after their employment as hereinafter provided, for political reasons, or for any other reasons than for dishonesty, inefficiency, insubordination, or habitual discourtesy to the public. To the end that efficiency and faithful service may be encouraged, the salaries of all clerks and employees in all departments of the city government hereinafter mentioned shall be fixed and regulated upon a graduated scale, by which such salaries shall be increased by length of service faithfully rendered."

[1] For a full explanation of the Chicago civil service system, see Second Annual Report of the Civil Service Commission to his Honor, the Mayor, for the year 1896; and also a paper by Mr.

ceiving the highest total placed first on the list from which appointments are made. This has been called Governor Black's scheme for "emasculating" the constitutional civil service provisions. The importance of the examination system in the civil service of great cities can hardly be overestimated. With appointments to subordinate positions made according to merit, the back of the spoils system is broken, and a new era is opened in the political life of our great cities. It is not probable that the recent setbacks which civil service reform seems to have experienced in Chicago and New York will be permanent. The experience of cities in other parts of the world is against the spoils system. In German and French cities the system of civil service examinations has generally excluded partisan politics from the appointment of subordinate officers, and it may be safely said that in so far as municipal government abroad has succeeded it has been based on the theory of appointments according to ascertained merit.

§ 114. **Legislative powers of the departments.** — It has already been stated that several of the commissions at the head of New York city administrative departments have some legislative power.[1] The board of health is, perhaps, a

Merritt Starr, published in the *Proceedings of the Baltimore Conference for Good City Government*, pp. 162-191.

[1] *Ante*, pp. 187, 188.

more important legislative body than the board of aldermen in the present city of New York. The ordinance powers of administrative departments are generally limited to making rules and regulations governing the subordinate officers and protecting the public property under the control of the departments concerned. Thus the police, fire, and street-cleaning departments issue a body of rules which the police officers, the firemen, and the street cleaners are bound to obey. A school board may pass ordinances for the care of school buildings or for regulating the processes of instruction. A dock commission may issue by-laws governing the use of the docks. A board of park commissioners may adopt rules which are in force only in the parks. In this way special ordinances are passed by an individual department which apply to the general body of citizens only as they come in contact with the sphere of this particular department. The ordinances of the board of health, the rules of the department of street cleaning in regard to the preparation of garbage and ashes for the cartmen, the ordinances of the water commissioners governing the distribution of water and fixing the water rents, and perhaps some other kinds of legislative action by department heads affect practically all of the people and thus become general rather than special in character. The plan of granting important legislative powers to the heads of departments is most fully developed in the United States and Germany. In France the department chiefs are responsible to the mayor, while in England the council committees have to report all of their plans to the council as a whole for its approval.

§ 115. Importance of the study of individual departments. — The government of cities is coming to be of such vast moment, and municipal enterprises are undertaken on such a large scale and involve so great an expenditure of money and effort, that the time is already here when a detailed study of the work of the administrative departments of a great metropolis is a necessary and absorbing task. The territorial organization of the administrative work of a city has been considered in the sections dealing with the division of the city into districts.[1] This problem of territorial organization involves some of the most fundamental principles of administrative and political science. Neighborhood lines are blotted out by the mere physical density of city populations. How are artificial boundaries to be made which will furnish a satisfactory substitute for natural boundaries? But aside from the matter of territorial organization, any great city department offers large opportunity for profitable study. Thus special attention should be given to the ways and means by which the department of finance exercises its control over the receipt and the expenditure of public money.

[1] *Ante*, pp. 138–143.

How are assessments made? How is the city property managed? How are contracts let? How are the employees of a city paid? How are the books kept? How is the auditing done? How are reports prepared? And again, in the department of street cleaning, the practical administrator, as well as the student of the methods and purposes of city government, may study with profit the organization of the force of sweepers and cartmen, and the methods of sweeping, of collecting wastes, and of the final disposition of refuse. An important problem in any department where a large body of workmen are employed by the city is the maintenance of friendly relations between the laborers and the officials of the department. In New York city Colonel Waring has been particularly successful in the solution of this problem so far as the street-cleaning department is concerned. The sweepers and cartmen are organized into forty-one sections, each of which has a representative on a general committee of employees. Before this "Committee of Forty-one" all complaints of unfair treatment are presented by the workmen and discussed at the committee's weekly sessions. A large proportion of the complaints made get no further than this committee. If, however, any complaint demands further consideration, it is laid before a committee of ten, five of whose members are representatives of the workmen and the five others representatives of the commissioner. Over this committee a workman always presides. The chief clerk of the department, one of the commissioner's representatives, is secretary. This committee of ten has the power to settle all disputes brought before it, if its members can agree. Otherwise a hearing is given before the commissioner himself, and the two sides of the case are presented by the chairman and the secretary of the committee of ten. It was recently announced that out of 245 complaints made during the first year this system was in vogue, all but one had been amicably settled without any appeal to the commissioner. This is merely one illustration of the far-reaching issues that are often involved in the details of departmental organization. The police department, the department of public works, the department of health, and many other individual departments furnish opportunity for almost unlimited study. In European cities where municipal activity is more varied and socialistic than in the United States, chemistry, physics, botany, zoölogy, bacteriology, mathematics, engineering, and almost the whole list of the natural and the mathematical sciences are made to contribute visibly to the art of municipal government. It is only in the study of the details of departmental work that one begins to see the richness and the universality of the problems of municipal administration. Even economics, sociology, ethics, and psychology have a direct and constant influence upon the organization of governmental activity. This influence is seen most clearly, and is most palpable in the minute details.

VI. *The City Judiciary*

§ 116. Judicial organization in cities. — It will not be possible to consider in great detail the organization of municipal courts and of the local divisions of general courts. The administration of justice has become so far nationalized in modern times, that the organization of local courts is often considered as lying outside the sphere of city charters and city authorities. Yet the great importance that attached to city courts in the middle ages has not been wholly lost. The multiplication of social relations and business transactions, as well as the existence of a special body of city laws, makes a great increase of litigation probable in any large municipality. Even to-day, in spite of the centralization that has been going on in judicial administration, almost every city of any importance has its municipal or corporation court. Thus we may distinguish two kinds of courts in cities. First, there are these strictly corporation courts, and second, there are the local courts which form a part of the regular system of state or national judicial organization.

§ 117. Corporation courts. — The strictly municipal or corporation courts may be civil, criminal, or police courts. The jurisdiction of municipal civil and criminal courts is generally limited to unimportant cases. The trial of offences against city ordinances, which used to be the main function of the mayor's or recorder's court, is now sometimes attended to by the regular local courts, since the position of the city has been changed from that of a close corporation to that of a local agent of the general government or the state. A study of the borough and city courts in England prior to the municipal reform of 1835, and in the City of London even at the present day, would reveal, perhaps better than anything else surviving in the nineteenth century, the nature of city government under the feudal system.[1] But for the purpose of coming to understand present conditions, a study of the police courts would be more important than a study of the other municipal courts. Wherever there is a regular uniformed police force, there is almost sure to be some kind of a police court, which is usually held by a judge or magistrate called a police justice. In Salt Lake City the police justice is appointed by the city council from among the justices of the peace elected by the people. The charter of Springfield, Mass., provides for a police court, "to consist of one learned and discreet person to be appointed and commissioned by the governor, pursuant to the

[1] See J. R. Somers Vine, *English Municipal Institutions*, pp. 127-184; and Firth, *Municipal London*, pp. 134-140.

constitution, to take cognizance of all crimes, offences, and misdemeanors committed within the city whereof justices of the peace now have, or may hereafter have, jurisdiction."[1] This court has been given jurisdiction in civil cases involving as much as $300, in lunacy cases, and in cases of juvenile offenders.[2] The charter of the city of Rochester, passed in 1880, provided that no more justices of the peace should be elected within the city, but that there should be a municipal court, to be composed of two judges chosen by the people. The jurisdiction of this court was described in detail.[3] In New York city the office of police justice was abolished by an act of 1895, and a board of city magistrates established instead. The old system had degenerated into a mockery of justice and an engine of oppression. In Paris there is an officer, called the police commissary, in every quarter of the city. This officer is said to be the descendant of the neighborhood arbiter of former centuries. His present duties are to decide cases of arrest, and prepare prosecutions for the regular courts.[4]

§ 118. **Local courts of the general judicial system.** — In this class are district courts, probate

---

[1] Charter of 1852, sect. 22.

[2] The Revised Ordinances of the City of Springfield, 1890, p. 23, note.

[3] Laws of New York, 1880, Chap. 14, Title X., sect. 245.

[4] See Shaw, *Municipal Government in Continental Europe*, pp. 42–44: and Block and Pontich, *op. cit.*, pp. 769–774.

courts, general and special sessions of the peace, and all the list of local courts provided by the judicial system of each country. Of course, the aggregation of great populations into small areas multiplies and changes the character of litigation to a great degree. One author, describing the municipal administration of Prussia during the twelfth century, says that a city was distinguished by three things, — the market right, the city wall, and the city law.[1] When law was chiefly a matter of custom or merely the natural outgrowth of social relationships, the simple "land law" which governed the relations of the peasants was plainly insufficient for the burghers of the cities with their greater complexity of social and commercial activities. Thus there came to be a "city law" as well as a "land law." This required a separate system of courts, for the judges were not professional, and the peasants knew only the "land law," while the burghers knew only the "city law." With the development of a body of written law and the advent of a professional class of lawyers and judges, the original cause for the differentiation of municipal courts was partly removed, and the constant tendency of modern judicial administration has been in the direction of uniformity and central control. This process of development can be seen in the history of the courts of New York city. New York's early charters were essentially mediæ-

[1] See Bornhak, *Geschichte der Preussischen Verwaltungsrecht.*

val and feudal. A system of special corporation courts was developed and took such deep root in the framework of the city government that it was the constitution of 1894 which first extended the general judicial system of the state over New York city to the exclusion of the old local corporation courts. In 1846, when a city charter convention and a state constitutional convention were sitting at the same time, the problem of the city's judicial organization was discussed. The committee of the city convention on the judiciary, in a long report describing the historical development of the city courts, took ground against any interference by the state convention with the special organization of the judiciary in the city. Speaking of the higher courts of civil jurisdiction, the committee declared that they could not but "foresee, in the breaking up of a local system, which has worked, and is working, so successfully as ours, a degree of embarrassment in the transaction of legal business in this city, which would more than counterbalance any benefits which the substitution of a new judicial establishment could possibly carry with it." Speaking of the marine court and the assistant justices' courts, which were the other local courts of civil jurisdiction, the committee went on to say that "these courts are also the subject of charter creation, and of both constitutional and statutory regulation, peculiar entirely to themselves; and while a great diversity of opinion exists in the community as to the expediency of their being continued in their present form, the committee believe that none whatever exists as to the propriety of retaining the inferior court establishment of this city, in such form as the people of this city, represented in this convention, may approve." In regard to the branch of the local judiciary with criminal jurisdiction, the committee said: "It consists of the courts of oyer and terminer, of general and special sessions, and the police courts. The first of these has general criminal jurisdiction; the second has jurisdiction of all cases less than capital; the third, a summary jurisdiction in cases of a minor character; and the fourth has cognizance of all original complaints, and special powers in regard to cases of vagrancy, bastardy, etc. Their functions are regulated by provisions peculiarly applicable to the wants of this city, and while the committee are very willing to admit that they are all susceptible of great improvement, they cannot but believe that that improvement should still continue the subject of local regulation."[1] This protest against state interference in the city judicial organization was successful for the time, but that interference was inevitable in the long run. It is to supplant an old system of corporation courts or to supply the judicial needs of a city just come into existence that local divisions of the general judiciary are

[1] See Proceedings of City Convention of 1846, pp. 115–123.

established in cities. The discussion of the organization of such local courts belongs to the study of general local administration, and need not be expanded in an outline of the special problems of city government.

§ 119. **Appointment and tenure of judicial officers.**
— The tenure of the judges is one of the most important points in any judicial system. For the purposes of public as well as private law it is considered requisite in England and the United States that judicial officers should be independent of the executive and legislative authorities except in case of gross and plain violation of duty. Hence judges are usually appointed for life, or elected directly by the people for a term of years. Sometimes, however, local judicial officers are appointed and removed by the central government at pleasure. Thus, in England, on petition of a borough council, the Queen may appoint a stipendiary magistrate for any borough, to hold office during Her Majesty's pleasure.[1] But in case of vacancy by dismissal or otherwise, another magistrate can be appointed only after a new petition has been made by the council. Where there is a recorder in an English town, he is appointed by the Crown to hold during good behavior.[2] In the city municipalities of British Columbia every police magistrate is appointed by the lieutenant-governor in council, and

---

[1] English Municipal Code, 1882, sect. 161.
[2] *Ibid.*, sect. 163.

holds during the pleasure of the appointing power.[1] In the commonwealths of the United States, judges, both state and local, are usually elected for a term of years. But in New York city the city magistrates and the judges of special sessions are appointed by the mayor for a term of ten years. The recorder, the city judge, and the judges of general sessions are elected for terms of fourteen years, while the judges of the district courts are elected for terms of six years. All of these judicial officers are excepted from the mayor's power of removal in New York. The recorders who are the judges of the four police courts of New Orleans are elected every four years.[2] In Wilmington, Del., the city judge, who presides over the municipal court, is appointed by the governor of the state for twelve years.[3] In 1892 a local court of civil jurisdiction was established in the city of Syracuse, N.Y.[4] There were to be two judges, appointed by the governor, not more than one of them to belong to the same political party. The terms of office of these judges were to be five and six years respectively, and their successors were to be elected by the people.

§ 120. **Judicial procedure.** — One of the most important guarantees of civil liberty under any

[1] The Municipal Clauses Act, 1896, sect. 199.
[2] City Charter of 1896, sects. 68, 69.
[3] Manual of the Council, 1896, p. 62.
[4] Laws of New York, 1892, Chap. 342.

government is the establishment of certain fixed forms of judicial procedure. For the practical attainment of public justice citizens must have the opportunity to become familiar with the methods of claiming and procuring the protection of the courts. It is customary in city charters, where the corporation is given powers over the lives and property of the citizens, to limit the exercise of these powers by laying out in detail the procedure which the corporation must use. This is particularly true in matters relating to taxation, assessment for benefits, and eminent domain. In these and other fields the city must often have recourse to judicial authorities for the enforcement of its rights, and the citizen practically always, in America at least, has recourse to courts for protection against governmental aggressions. For minor offences against the public peace and good order in cities, magistrates and police judges may try and convict citizens by "summary process," that is, without a jury and the usual formalities which delay judicial trials and give the citizen the fullest opportunity for self-defence. The discussion of judicial procedure in its details must be left to the professional lawyer. Indeed, it is the intricacy of the ways and means of obtaining justice in the different courts established in a great city that makes the legal profession so necessary to every citizen who has rights to defend or claims to enforce. The citizen becomes dependent upon the lawyers just in proportion as litigation is multiplied and the organization of the judiciary is complicated by the existence of numerous courts with different or concurrent jurisdiction and different rules of procedure. In New York city the city magistrates form a board which has power to adopt rules governing the city magistrates' courts.[1]

§ 121. **Ministerial officers of the judiciary.** — It is through these ministerial officers, such as constables, sheriffs, marshals, and the like, that the judicial authorities are enabled to enforce their will by use of the physical power of the government. The constable is the local peace officer at the basis of the English and American systems. This fact has had the effect in England of causing the regular police force of the cities to be called the "constabulary." Police officers generally have the authority of constables in keeping the peace and making arrests. The sheriff is a county officer. The marshal is a city officer, generally directly under the mayor's authority. The city marshal is sometimes called the mayor's marshal, and was originally the ministerial officer to the mayor as chief magistrate of the city. Now the marshal's duties have been somewhat altered. In New York city his chief function at the present time is to grant licenses in the name of the mayor for pushcarts, pawnbrokers, pedlers, etc. The city marshal of Albany is appointed by the mayor subject

[1] Laws of New York, 1895, Chap. 601.

to rejection by the council. The marshal's duties are to act as sergeant-at-arms to the council and obey the instructions of the mayor. In a good many of the smaller cities the marshal is elected. This is the case, for example, in Grand Rapids, Mich., where the marshal's term of office is two years. In Springfield, Mass., the city marshal is at the head of the police department and receives his appointment from the mayor and aldermen. In Greater New York there will be ten marshals appointed by the mayor for terms of six years. Among the ministerial officers of the judicial organization should be mentioned the public administrator. There is such an officer in New York, Brooklyn, and San Francisco. In New York city the public administrator was, until 1895, a subordinate of the corporation counsel. He now has an independent bureau and is appointed by the surrogates of the county.[1]

§ 122. **Public prosecution.**[2] — In treating of the judicial organization in cities reference should be made to the public prosecutor. In the United States he is primarily a county officer, and is known as the district or prosecuting attorney. It

[1] See New York City Consolidation Act, 1882, sect. 216; and Laws of New York, 1895, Chap. 827.

[2] For a full discussion of the general principles of private and public prosecution, with a particular description of the American district attorney, see Professor Goodnow's chapter on "Control of the Criminal Courts," *Comparative Administrative Law*, Vol. II., pp. 178-189.

is largely within his discretion whether he shall prosecute offenders against the law or not. This discretion is particularly dangerous in cases relating to official violation of duty. A public prosecutor elected by a political party is under strong temptation to use his office to protect other officers of his own party. Where the spoils system gets control of the government of a city, as was the case in New York under Tammany Hall, the office of district attorney comes to be one of the most important offices in the whole local system for the furtherance of partisan ends. The district attorney of New York county is elected for a term of four years. The district attorney in Philadelphia is elected every three years. This officer is primarily a representative of the central government, though elected by the people of the locality. In Glasgow, Scotland, the public prosecutor in the police courts is called the " Procurator Fiscal of Police."

§ 123. **The jury system.** — One of the fundamental obligations of citizenship in countries where civil liberty is guaranteed is jury service. This obligation was more easily fulfilled in earlier Anglo-Saxon communities, where population was not large and the pressure of modern life was not yet felt, than it is to-day, especially in our large cities. It is unnecessary in a treatise on the study of city government to describe the origin or even the present status of the jury system. Such a description may be left to a more general work on government. But attention should be called to the increased difficulty of the problem of jury service in cities. In the first place, there are more exemptions. All city officials in New York whose duties would interfere with serving on juries are exempt. This one exemption applies to the thousands of policemen, firemen, street cleaners, and schoolteachers. There are many other exemptions, such as of United States officers, pilots, railway employees, officers of vessels, the members of certain professions, etc., which apply to a larger proportion of the residents of a city than of a rural district. The requirement that a juror must possess a certain amount of property in his own or in his wife's name, also bars more people in the city than in the country, where wealth is more equally distributed. If to this be added the fact that a large proportion of the citizens of an American city subject to jury service are of foreign extraction and do not in all cases appreciate the meaning of the jury system in the general theory of local self-government, it can easily be seen that the jury problem is a difficult one to solve in cities like New York, Chicago, or San Francisco. The pressure of private business is so great in the case of many who are called to serve on the jury that they are willing to adopt almost any method to escape the duty. Jury service is not usually inviting to a man of culture or a man in active business life, and the nominal wages of the juror makes service a considerable financial sacrifice to persons in lucrative employment. The result is a strong temptation to the use of money for the purchase of exemptions. By paying a fee into the hands of the clerk of court, influence may sometimes be brought to bear upon the judge to have the juror excused. The result is a subtle corrupting of the general judicial administration which is fatal to the best work of government. In New York city there is a commissioner of jurors, who receives a salary of $5000 per year. In 1895 there was turned into the sinking fund from his office the small sum of $1295, which had been paid in as fines and forfeitures for failure to perform jury duty. Of course, a multiplicity of courts and a great divergence in their judicial procedure add to the complexity of the jury problem.

§ 124. **Centralization of responsibility in municipal government.** — It seems that during recent years municipal reformers in the United States have made it their chief purpose to get responsibility centralized in the hands of one man, the mayor. This policy marks a natural reaction from the plan of diffused responsibility which had obtained so extreme a development in American cities. The spoils system is bad enough under any circumstances when applied to municipal administration. But when, combined with the spoils system, we find a conglomerate mass of unrelated authorities, of all degrees of independence, then we certainly have city government under the worst conditions. A confusion of responsibility means little or no responsibility at all. It is not strange that reformers have revolted against the old system which provided a separate and independent board or officer for each of the city departments, and gave the council the means of doing mischief with very little opportunity for doing anything good. The remedy to which charter-makers have been looking is the concentration of responsibility. It is argued that the people can choose one man fit to govern, better than they can choose a number of men of like fitness. The voters have been confused by the long list of officers for whom they have been compelled to vote. By concentrating responsibility in the hands of one man, the citizens can keep their attention fixed upon him and bring public opinion to bear upon his action. In the worst case the people can refuse to reëlect an officer who has not measured up to the demands made upon him by his constituents. It seems clear that the basis of this agitation for the concentration of power in the hands of one man is the belief that our city governments have suffered more from the rascality than from the incapacity of those in power. It is the old struggle to array the "good" citizens against the "bad" in political warfare. This movement takes for one of its premises that the people themselves are "good," but that they have been hoodwinked by professional plunderers through the manipulation of a bad system of political organization. As a matter of fact, the people are not very good, and in many cases they do not want very good government. At best they want good government only now and then. The citizens of our cities would be very glad to get something for nothing. They would be glad to have a government that would be good to them as individuals and that would cost them nothing of time or effort or money. The very fact that the "municipal dictator" system of city government is just now so popular with the American public goes to show that the people are not in general good citizens. Of course, it could not be safely maintained that a government in a free country is always as good as the people deserve. Sometimes the dead weight of an outgrown system in the hands of a clique cannot easily be thrown off. In such cases the general tone of citizenship is likely to be higher than the tone of government. On the other hand, when the people have been galled by oppression until they do throw off the yoke of inefficient and corrupt government, it may often happen that the "reform" administration brought into power on the flood tide of public feeling will give the people a better government than they deserve. This is seen in the revulsion of the masses of a great city against "reform" after it has once been tried. It is possible that too much attention has been paid in municipal political movements to rascality in official conduct, and too little attention to incompetence. This mistake is made by the advocates of the dictatorial mayor system of municipal government. Honesty as against dishonesty can never be a permanent or healthy issue between political parties. Those who wish to concentrate all power and responsibility in the mayor's hands seem to think that any one chosen by popular vote must be capable of efficient administration, if he is kept constantly under the public gaze. This is the egotism of democracy. But the experience of the world goes far to disprove the correctness of this belief. A man cannot be taken from the merchant's store or from the workman's bench and be turned into an efficient administrator by the simple magic of popular election by free citizens of a great republic. The best experience of the states of Europe is distinctly opposed to the one-man power in municipal government. Outside of the United States the council is everywhere the central authority of the city. In England the committees of the council absorb even the executive and administrative functions of the corporation. German municipal administration is carried on by boards. In France, to be sure, the mayor is vested with the whole executive authority of the commune, but he is put under a strong central control. There is some danger that the American movement for concentration of power may degenerate into a "fad." Centralization of responsibility seems to be something of a makeshift for the personal political responsibility of the general body of citizens. It is the effort of the people to get some one to govern them and thus avoid the trouble of self-government. Most of the work of city government is of such a nature that it requires deliberation in planning and coöperation in execution. And the simple fact that the masses of citizens in every large city in the United States are so heterogeneous as to be unfitted for present coöperation, though their interests are one, renders the concentration of power in the hands of a single officer a seemingly necessary makeshift in the evolution of free government, to be accepted for the present with the hope of a change in the direction of real democracy, when the social and political ideals of the strangely mingled populations of our cities have been fused and unified. In other words, the cause of the necessity for the "prodigious power of the mayor"[1]

---

[1] The *Brooklyn Daily Eagle* of May 6, 1897, contained a diagram showing "The Prodigious Power of the Mayor of Greater New York." The first mayor will have the absolute power of appointment to more than 70 positions, the salaries of which range from $5000 to $15,000 per year. Every succeeding mayor, elected for a full term, can remove all of these officers during his first six months of incumbency, if he desires, and appoint their successors. Besides these principal officers, there are a large number who receive smaller salaries, and nearly 100 unsalaried commissioners, all of whom are to be appointed by the mayor.

is the lack of a civic consciousness, a consciousness of unified interests among the citizens. The people do not realize their own need of political coöperation, or, if they realize the need, they feel their unfitness.

§ 125. Purpose of organization in government. — The central purpose of political organization is to fix responsibility. Organization, indeed, is the fixing of responsibility. This does not necessarily mean the concentration of responsibility. It is true that in order to have a full utilization of energy a simple organization is needed. But, after all, organization means the fitting of all the parts into their proper places, their complete coördination and subordination, so that each shall stand for what it is worth, for what it can do. As a result of these facts, it is wholly impossible to say *a priori* what form of municipal organization is best. In every system and under all conditions, organization has this one aim, — the placing of responsibility. And as responsibility can be placed only where there is capacity to respond to the demands made, it appears that forms of organization are to be determined in every case by the character and capacity of the people to be organized. That form of organization is best which, under the existing conditions of public intelligence, public experience, civic spirit, and common honesty prevailing in each particular city, succeeds best in making the whole body of public authorities, from the chief magistrate to the humblest elector, individually and collectively responsible for the good government of the municipality. If democracy is to be a success, all those who participate in sovereignty must have freedom, tempered with a sense of responsibility. The citizen must be organized into the government, and not the government organized over the citizen. Perhaps the strong mayoralty is the staff upon which an American city must lean until the people come to know each other better and grow into civic unity. But as time goes on, and the problems of our new civilization approach nearer and nearer to solution, we shall doubtless find a form of organization as well fitted to the strength of the civic unity of that day as the concentration of power is fitted to the weakness and division of this day's citizenship.

CHAPTER V

CONCLUDING REMARKS

§ 126. Fundamental unity of the city with the whole system of government. — There has been presented on these pages simply a classified enumeration of the problems of city government, with such suggestions as were intended to show the wide scope and the absorbing interest of a comprehensive study of municipal tasks and forms of organization. From the standpoint of administrative law, the degree of isolation in which the city has been put for the purposes of this outline would scarcely be justified. It is always necessary to reserve in our consciousness the fundamental fact that the city as an agent of government is a part of a general system from which it cannot be separated. Almost all the functions of city government are simply the functions of ordinary local or general government intensified. Even the complexity of life resulting from the aggregation of people in cities is only one phase of the complexity of all life brought about by modern industrial and social conditions. In no direction can we isolate the city for purposes of study, if we mean by isolation the severance of outside relations. The importance of the field, however, and the limited amount of work that any one person or class of persons can do, make it necessary in a comprehensive scheme of political science, constitutional law, and administration to admit a considerable delimitation of the field for special studies.

§ 127. **Present reasons for isolating the city.** — If we grant the necessity of specialization in our study of the several areas of governmental organization, there is no part of the whole field which, at this particular period of political development, can better be set aside for detailed study than local government in cities. It is here that the reconstruction of political practice and of social institutions goes on most rapidly. Here we find the most extensive and natural encroachment of the government on the field of private initiative. It is more than likely that if socialism ever comes, it will come by way of the city; that is, the way will lead up to general socialism by the steady enlargement of municipal functions. The city has in its hands the expenditure of vast sums of public money. The annual income and expenditure of the municipalities that make up Greater New York aggregate about $80,000,000, or more than three times the total annual expenditure of New York state. The ordinary yearly budget of Paris amounts to about $60,000,000. The expenditure of public money for water supply, streets, sewers, parks, docks, etc., is extraordinarily great in cities. And the rapid growth of wealth, as well as the variety of its forms, makes the problem of taxation especially serious in the city. In every respect it may be said that the city furnishes an intensification of the governmental problems. The cities are the nerve-centres of the social, industrial, and political world. In the cities we find the best and latest fruits of civilization side by side with the dregs of associated life. The social waste, which Professor Giddings calls the cost of progress,[1] the rubbish and the wreckage that come from the wear and tear due to the friction in social organization, are sure to accumulate in great centres of population. The problem of the disposal of physical wastes and of the waste portions of humanity is in reality the most acute problem of municipal activity.[2]

§ 128. City conditions as they affect the political capacity of the citizens. — Back of the merely political problems of the city lie the great problems

---

[1] See "The Ethics of Social Progress," a chapter contributed to the book *Philanthropy and Social Progress*, edited by Professor Henry C. Adams.

[2] The writer is indebted to Dr. Lewis G. Janes, author of *The Problem of City Government*, and to Mr. Edmond Kelly, founder of the City Club of New York, author of *Evolution and Ethics*, and lecturer on *Municipal Politics* in Columbia University, for the idea that the key-problem of city government is the disposal of both physical and human wastes.

of social development. Of course, government depends for its success upon the capacity and loyalty of those who have a part in the work of governing. If the city makes its citizens more intelligent and more loyal to the interests of the community in which they live, then we may believe that urban life itself helps to solve the problems it creates. But there seems to be reason for the fear that, in spite of the culture and wealth and activity of the city, in spite of the development of the highest forms of social life in the city, in spite of the noblest works of civilization found there, the average capacity of the inhabitants for thought and action is at least no greater than it is in rural districts. There is no reason to dispute that the friction of social contact gives to the ordinary city man a certain polish and superficial intelligence which are lacking in most countrymen. A product of the slums can board a street-car more nimbly than many an intelligent farmer. The most important accomplishment of a citizen according to the conscious or unconscious standards of the inhabitants of a great city is that he be " up to date." He must read the news to-day, even though to-morrow he may read that it was not so. To be "up to date" in this sense is no proof of intelligence, certainly no proof of political capacity. It is certainly true that the craving for excitement and the nervous tension resulting from modern conditions in general, and from urban conditions in particular, tend to impair the capacity of the people for study and reflection by consuming their time and dissipating their energy. Perhaps it could be shown that there are great compensating advantages, but the disadvantages are indisputable. And from this standpoint the haste of urban life tends to endanger the popular fitness for political power and responsibility. Democracy must fight for its life in the cities; for it is not sufficient that the people of cities should merely have as great political capacity as their contemporaries in the country. In order that democracy shall succeed, the political capacity of the people must increase in proportion to the increased difficulty of the problems of government.

§ 129. **Social disintegration in cities.** — But not only is there danger of the impairment of individual capacity through the constraining influence of city conditions. The fundamental units of social organization also suffer change. The family and the neighborhood may be considered the units of society from which nations and states are built. But in the great city of the nineteenth century, with its rapid transportation facilities and its quickly shifting elements of population, neighborhood life is almost annihilated, and the family itself suffers a great change in the direction of looser ties and more scattered interests. Among the masses who live in tenement houses and use common halls, common yards, common water and lighting facilities, and a common street in front of a common doorway, there is no encouragement to the privacy and sacredness of home life. The very lack of room compels the residents of the crowded districts of a city like New York to herd in the streets and in the public squares and parks. With persons belonging to the middle class conditions are somewhat better and not quite so fatal to home life. But even they must live in flats or apartment houses, or if they have a whole house to themselves, they must take in boarders out of sheer necessity to help pay the enormous rents. An ordinary house in a clean street in New York city where the middle classes live brings $1000 a year rent to the owner. Of course it is only in cities where population is very dense that rents are so high. In Philadelphia, Chicago, and the smaller cities of America, a much greater proportion of families can live by themselves than in New York. But the families of the very wealthy everywhere are to some extent disintegrated by the presence of a retinue of hired servants. Thus among people of all classes genuine home life in the historic sense is impossible or very greatly obstructed under metropolitan conditions. It is not yet easy to see what the ultimate effect of the disintegration of home and neighborhood life will be upon the political organization of cities and the capacity of the citizens for self-government. This question is a vital one in the interpretation of the meaning of present-day movements and the probable future course of development of political and social institutions.

§ 130. Cities and the progress of civilization. — We are coming face to face with the question of the ebb and flow of civilization. It is beginning to dawn upon us that perhaps we are not "on the home stretch" of human progress. Perhaps even yet we may have war and ruin and a dark age. We are told that "history repeats itself." The question is whether the human race has grown wise enough from its experience to guide the future course of society so that history shall not repeat its blunders. It is difficult to see the ultimate advantages of civilization unless it contributes to the foresight and directing power of man in his social organization. But we all know that one of man's most marvellous characteristics is his ability to forget and ignore past experience. Of the lessons we go over we retain only the merest fraction, and the evolution of social wisdom is a slow and painful process of the repetition of experiences, of which the great majority seem to be lost. Are we at the flood tide of civilization? Does an ebb come next? These questions depend for their answer especially, it may well be, upon the political wisdom brought to bear upon the problems of the city. The expansion of the functions of municipal government for the protection of public safety and public health is certainly inevitable. Must the economic and idealistic functions of municipal government expand in like manner? Hon. John Boyd Thatcher, mayor of Albany, has said:[1] "If the city may do those things for the individual which he cannot do for himself, may it do for him those things which he finds it inconvenient to do for himself? If it may care for his safety and his health, may it also care for his morals and his comforts? If it may build him an academy to educate a sound mind, may it build him a gymnasium to develop a sound body? If it build him a gymnasium to train his muscles, may it erect an arena to test his prowess? If it publish police rules and regulations for his conduct, may it establish an ethical college to teach him the foundation of obligation? If it may teach him ethics, may it teach him religion? And may all these things be done at public expense? Here our vessel breaks from its moorings and drifts toward the beautiful but dangerous coast of paternal government." The experience of many cities has proven beyond a doubt that the municipal ownership and management of transportation lines, waterworks, lighting works, markets, docks, and other works rendering common public service may be of immediate advantage to the public under some conditions. But is this advantage reaped at the expense of the future? Do the economic undertakings of gov-

---

[1] See an article on "The Citizen and his City," published in the *Arena*, Vol. XVII., p. 854 (May, 1897).

ernment only emphasize the failure of government to govern? These are social questions, and must be answered by the sovereign body in each country of the world.

§ 131. **Concluding summary of political problems.** — The more immediate political questions we have grouped under the problems of control and the problems of organization. In solving the former, our task is to maintain a sufficient equilibrium in political institutions and political activity between the various elements of society. The fever of city life must be tempered. City and country must be held together politically. The unity of political relations must be maintained. The distinguishing forces of intensified local life must be resisted. Then with the problems of the organization of political institutions in cities, we find a splendid opportunity to prove the worth of our political wisdom and the effective value of our past experience. Organization, as has been said, is the placing of responsibility. How shall we direct the forces of city life so that they may strengthen and not weaken the political capacity of the people? Municipal government is a delicate task. It demands the highest wisdom of the state as well as the best abilities of citizens in all the fields of science and art. In some way the unconscious multitudes must be brought to understand how absorbingly interesting municipal problems are in every direction. Competition for the attention of city men is very sharp. Government must enter into the struggle with all its resources. Organization must be so perfected as to present in every possible way to the citizens its claims for their enthusiastic attention. Democracy is at stake.

LIST OF AUTHORITIES CITED IN THIS VOLUME.

Adams, Prof. H. C., *Philanthropy and Social Progress*, 236.
Allinson and Penrose, *Philadelphia*, 175.
American Academy of Political and Social Science, *Annals*, 34, 84, 86.
Arena, 241.
Arnold, *Roman Provincial Administration*, 101.
Ashley, Prof. W. J., *Economic History*, 76.

Baltimore conference for good city government, Proceedings, 43, 59, 113, 151, 164, 200, 209.
Belgium, *Constitution*, 79.
Bell, Sir James, and Paton, James, *Glasgow: its Municipal Organization and Administration*, 95, 133, 159.
Block and Pontich, *Administration de la Ville de Paris*, 45, 50, 96, 137, 138, 146, 216.
Booth, Mary L., *History of New York City*, 174.
Bornhak, *Geschichte des Preussischen Verwaltungsrechts*, 96, 98, 217.
British Columbia, *The Municipal Clauses Act of 1896*, 221.
Brooklyn Daily Eagle, 231.

Bryce, James, *The American Commonwealth*, 67, 126.
Burgess, Prof. J. W., *Political Science and History*, 2; *Political Science and Constitutional Law*, 17, 78.

California, *Constitution*, 84.
Chicago, *Second Annual Report of the Civil Service Commission*, 208.
Colorado, *Constitution*, 83.
Columbia College, *Studies in History, Economics, and Public Law*, 59, 97.
Commons, Prof. J. R., *Proportional Representation*, 156.

Dareste de la Chavanne, *Histoire de l'Administration en France*, 2, 71, 102.
Davis, *The Municipal Condition of Atlanta*, 151.
Dolman, Frederick, *Municipalities at Work*, 29, 135.
Dongan, Gov. Thomas, *New York City Charter*, 42, 132.
Dublin, *Corporation Diary*, 125.
Dundee, *Corporation Accounts*, 18, 58.
Durand, Dr. E. Dana, *Political and Municipal Legislation in 1896*,

86; *The Finances of New York City*, 26, 59, 85, 165, 174.

Ecuador, *Constitution*, 79.
Educational Review, 101.
Emerick, C. F., *An Analysis of Agricultural Discontent in the United States*, 5.
England, *Municipal Code of* 1882, 102, 144, 157, 220; *Municipal Corporations Act of* 1835, 178.

Ferron, H. de, *Institutions municipales et provinciales comparées*, 17, 102, 128, 182, 188.
Firth, J. M. B., *Municipal London*, 25, 215.
Florida, *Constitution*, 106.
Fowler, Prof. W. W., *The City-State of the Greeks and Romans*, 1, 16, 59, 75.
France, *Municipal Code of* 1884, 68, 94, 97, 102, 150, 184, 186, 188.
Fustel de Coulanges, *The Ancient City*, 16.

German Empire, *Constitution*, 78.
Giddings, Prof. F. H., *The Ethics of Social Progress*, 236.
Gilbert, *The City*, 58, 135.
Glasgow, Lord Provost's *Résumé of New Work*, 18, 133.
Goodnow, Professor Frank J., 10, 11, 19, 20, 72, 156; *Comparative Administrative Law*, 10, 17, 96, 103, 144, 182, 184, 224; *Municipal Home Rule*, 10, 80, 103, 170, 186; *Municipal Problems*, 8, 10, 19, 20, 65, 70, 72, 96, 102, 103, 144, 156, 172, 186.
Great Britain, *Census Reports*, 138.
Greater New York, *Charter*, 106, 165, 187, 188.
Green, Mrs. J. R., *Town Life in the Fifteenth Century*, 2, 77.

Guthrie, George M., *The Municipal Condition of Pittsburg*, 59.
Hartford, *Municipal Register*, 183.
Hartog, Dr. L. de, *Das Staatsrecht des Königreichs der Niederlande*, 79.
Hawaiian Republic, *Letter from Foreign Office*, 93.
Holls, Hon. F. W., *State Boards of Control*, 113.
Honduras, *Constitution*, 80.
Howard, *The Recent Revolt in Baltimore*, 200.
Howe, *Municipal History of New Orleans*, 57, 148.

Illinois, *Constitution*, 91.
Indiana, *Supreme Court Reports*, "Crawfordsville *vs.* Braden," 21.
Interstate Commerce Commission, *Second Annual Report*, 4, 5.

Janes, Dr. Lewis G., *The Problem of City Government*, 25, 26, 30, 163, 236.
Jenks, Professor Edward, *The Government of Victoria*, 102, 105, 112, 120, 159.
Jewitt, Hon. E. B., *Mayor's Message*, 40.
Johns Hopkins University *Studies*, 57, 61, 97, 148.

Kelly, Edmond, *Evolution and Ethics*, 236.
Kent, Chancellor, *The Charter of the City of New York*, 84, 125.
Kentucky, *Constitution*, 83.

Leber, *Pouvoir Municipal*, 102.
Leidig, *Preussisches Staatsrecht*, 145, 146.
Levermore, *Town and City Government of New Haven*, 183.

LIST OF AUTHORITIES. 247

Louisiana, *Constitution*, 90; *Laws*, 149, 178, 221.

Maitland, F. W. (*see* Pollock and Maitland).
Maltbie, Milo R., *English Local Government of To-day*, 97, 98, 102, 111.
Mann, Henry, *Ancient and Mediæval Republics*, 17, 74, 75, 78, 98.
Marquardsen, Dr. Heinrich, *Handbuch des Oeffentlichen Rechts*, 79.
Maryland, *Constitution*, 90.
Massachusetts, *Laws*, 97.
Matthews, Hon. Nathan, Jr., *City Government of Boston*, 3, 26, 97, 195.
Mayor's Committee, New York city, *Report on Public Baths and Public Comfort Stations*, 46.
Michigan, *Constitution*, 82; *Laws*, 1865, 97; *General Statutes*, 107; *Supreme Court Reports*, "People vs. Hurlbut," 20, 82; "Allor vs. Wayne Co. Auditors," 27; "Detroit Park Commissioners vs. The Common Council," 82; "Att. Gen. vs. Board of Councilmen," 205.
Milliken, *Municipal Condition of San Francisco*, 151.
Minneapolis and Cleveland Conferences for Good City Government, *Proceedings*, 116, 151, 162.
Missouri, *Constitution*, 90.
Moffett, S. R., *Suggestions on Government*, 65.
Montana, *Constitution*, 83.
Montgomerie, Governor, New York city charter, 42.

New York city, *Consolidation Act*, 224; *City Convention of 1846, Proceedings*, 219.

New York state, *Assembly Documents*, 1849, 86; *Constitution*, 81, 88, 91, 99, 106; *Constitutional Convention of 1894*, *Manual, American Constitutions*, 80; *Court of Appeals Reports*, "Rathbone vs. Wirth," 21, 205; "People vs. Albertson," 27, 82; "People vs. Draper," 82; "Metropolitan Board of Health vs. Heister," 82; "Astor vs. The Mayor," 82; *Laws*, 1847, 85; 1849, 155, 200; 1853, 140; 1857, 97, 155, 201; 1864, 199; 1865, 97; 1866, 98; 1869, 155; 1880, 218; 1883, 150; 1888, 149, 150; 1891, 166; 1892, 221; 1895, 150, 223; 1896, 140; 1897 (see Greater New York Charter), 106.
New South Wales, *Laws*, 102, 120, 159.

Oberholzer, E. P., *Home Rule for American Cities*, 84.
Ohio, *Constitutional Convention Debates*, 1873-74, 136; *Laws*, 95, 97.
Overland Monthly, 129.

Paton, James (*see* Bell, Sir James and Paton, James).
Patten, Prof. Simon N., *A Theory of Social Forces*, 34.
Pennsylvania, *Constitution*, 83, 106.
Philadelphia, *Manual of Councils*, 135.
Pingree, Hon. H. S., 80; *Mayor's Messages*, 40, 98.
Pollard, James, *A Study in Municipal Government: The Corporation of Berlin*, 29, 96, 144, 145.
Pollock and Maitland, *History of the English Law*, 33, 98.
Poore, Ben: Perley, *Federal and State Constitutions*, 80.

Prussia, *Städte Ordnung*, 1853, 102.

Ramalho, A., *L'administration municipale en XIIIe siècle dans les villes de consulat*, 76.
Revue Générale d'Administration, 76.
Riis, Jacob A., *How the Other Half Lives*, 140; *The Children of the Poor*, 140.
Rosewater, Dr. Victor, *Special Assessments*, 59.

Salter, William M., *The Relation of a Municipality to Quasi-Public Corporations enjoying Municipal Franchises*, 43.
San Francisco, *Board of Freeholders' Proposed Charter*, 207.
Shaw, Dr. Albert, *Municipal Government in Great Britain*, 6, 29, 94, 96, 139, 144, 196; *Municipal Government in Continental Europe*, 29, 38, 39, 96, 122, 127, 128, 130, 131, 132, 137, 148, 157, 182, 184, 216.
Snow, *City Government of St. Louis*, 97.
Speirs, Dr. F. W., *The Street Railway System of Philadelphia*, 61.
Springfield, Mass., *Charter of* 1852, 216; *Revised Ordinances*, 1890, 216.
Stallard, J. H., *The Municipal Government of San Francisco*, 129.
Starr, Merritt, *Chicago's Civil Service Reform*, 209.

Sydney Morning Herald *Supplement*, 111.

Tenement House Committee of 1894, New York, *Report*, 8.
Thatcher, Hon. John Boyd, *The Citizen and His City*, 241.
Tolman, Dr. W. H., *Municipal Reform Movements in the United States*, 116.

United States, *Supreme Court Reports*, "Loan Association vs. Topeka," 38.

Vine, J. R. Somers, *English Municipal Institutions*, 33, 132, 215.
Virginia, *Constitution*, 83.

Warner, Amos G., *American Charities*, 34, 100.
Webb, Sydney, *The London Programme*, 7.
Webster, W. C., *Recent Centralizing Tendencies in State Educational Administration*, 101.
Whitten, Robert H., *The Assessment of Taxes in Chicago*, 8.
Wilcox, *Municipal Government in Michigan and Ohio*, 21, 80, 97, 98, 102, 196.
Wilmington, Del., *Manual of the Council*, 221.
Wisconsin, *Constitution*, 83, 106.
Withy and Griffin, publishers, *The Laws and Customs, Rights, Liberties, and Privileges of the City of London*, 33, 98.
Woodruff, Clinton Rogers, 116.
Wyoming, *Constitution*, 84.

GENERAL INDEX.

Achæan League, federal government of, 78.

Administrative control, methods of, 105; appointment and removal of officers, 105-108; issuance of instructions, 108; approval or rejection of local by-laws and projects, 108-110; appeals from local decisions, 110; financial aid to localities, 111-113; central administrative control in the United States, 113, 114.

Administrative courts, in continental Europe, 110.

Administrative departments, organization and powers of, 191-214; number and spheres of activity of departments, 193-196; relations of, to central authority of the corporation, 196-198; appointment of heads of departments, 198-201; term of service, 201, 202; boards and single commissioners, 202-206; organization of subordinate service, 206-209; legislative powers of departments, 209-211; study of individual departments, 211-214.

Administrative districts in cities, 138-141.

Age, a qualification for suffrage, 122.

Alabama, municipal tax-rate limited in, 90.

Albany, enumeration of council's powers in charter of, 171; compulsory official service in, 179; mayor's veto power in, 185; confirmation of mayor's appointments in, 200; police bill of, declared void, 205; city marshal's functions in, 223, 224.

Allegheny, term of mayor of, 183; department of public safety in, 193.

America (*see* United States).

Appeal, a method of judicial control, 104; a method of administrative control, 110.

Appointment of city officers, a means of central control, 105-108.

Approval of local by-laws and projects, a means of central control, 108-110.

Approvisionement of cities, 31, 32.

Areas of cities, examples, 8; central control over, 93-96.

Arkansas, special municipal legislation prohibited in, 88; municipal tax-rate limited in, 90.

Athens, ancient, special taxation in, 59; an independent state, 74; control over allies, 75.

Atlanta, election of aldermen by general ticket in, 151; meetings of council of, 164; term of mayor of, 183.

Audit, a secondary function of government, 65.

Australia (*see* also New South Wales and Victoria), grant of financial aid to municipalities in, 111; newness of cities in, 120; term of municipal councillors in, 161; election of mayors in, 182.

Austria, age qualification for suffrage in, 122; classes of electors in, 127, 157; effect of tax-paying qualification in, 129; professional men and the suffrage in, 130.

Baltimore, the McDonough grant, 57; special constitutional provisions for, 90, 91; sessions of council of, 168; term of mayor of, 183; salary of mayor of, 191; election of police board of, 199; boards of, appointed by the governor, 199; deadlock in municipal appointments of, 200.

Banking and bank regulation, a function of government, 38.

Baths, public, 46.

Belgium, municipal self-government in, 79; residence required for municipal suffrage in, 121; age and other qualifications in, 122; family condition affecting the suffrage in, 129; proportional representation in, 156; term of municipal councillors in, 161; appointment of mayors in, 182; position of mayors in, 184.

Berlin, area, 8; health administration, 29; *approvisionement*, 32; police in, 96; percentage of foreign-born in, 118; electors in, 127; size of council of, 161.

Bicameral council, 163-165.

Bipartisan boards, 203-206.

Birmingham, municipal technical schools, 48; municipal property and improvement scheme, 55.

Black, Gov. Frank S., of New York, 185, 208, 209.

Blandin, Judge E. J., 162.

Boston, area, 8; bounties to soldiers, 26; Mechanic Arts High School of, 48; police board, 97; percentage of foreign-born in, 118; school campaign in, 123; council of, 151; minority representation in, 152, 153; size of council of, 161; bicameral council in, 163; term of mayor of, 183; salary of mayor of, 191; administrative departments in, 194, 195; boards of, appointed by the governor, 199.

Boundaries of municipal corporations, central control over, 93, 96.

Bremen, in the German Empire, 17, 78; corporate bodies and the suffrage in, 131, 132, 156.

Bridgeport, minority representation in, 153, 154; term of mayor of, 183; mayor's veto power in, 185; bipartisan system in, 204.

British Columbia, woman suffrage in, 123; freehold qualification for municipal suffrage in, 124; nominating system in, 158, 160; police magistrates in, 220.

British Empire (*see also* England and Great Britain), age qualification for suffrage in, 122; sessions of municipal councils in, 168.

Bronx, The, borough of Greater New York, 142.

Brooklyn, excise revenues of, 61; department of buildings in, 63; vote on consolidation, 66; council committee on legislation, 67; Brooklyn Bridge, 68; charter convention, 85, 86; special constitutional provisions for, 90; metropolitan fire board, 97; metropolitan health board, 98; school officers appointed in, 124; borough of Greater New York, 142; aldermen of, 148, 151; size of council of, 161; board of estimate of, 162, 196; aldermen chosen at large in, 164; term of mayor of, 183; administrative departments in, 194; term of department heads in, 201; public administrator in, 224.

Brooklyn Bridge, built and managed by two cities, 68.

Budapest, public theatres in, 50; municipal property of, 55; municipal council of, 148; size of council of, 161.

Buffalo, potato-farms in, 40; election of councillors by general ticket in, 150; procedure in council of, 166; compulsory official service in, 179; term of mayor of, 183; mayor a member of the police board of, 189; department of public works in, 195; school government of, 203; bipartisan boards in, 205.

Burdens and benefits of government, 53, 54.

Business and politics in city government, 19-24, 37, 38.

By-laws, local — approval of, by central authorities, 108, 110.

California, special municipal commissions in, 84; formation of city charters in, 84; special municipal legislation prohibited in, 88; municipal indebtedness limited in, 90; educational qualification in, 130; size of legislature of, 163.

Cambridge, Mass., term of mayor of, 183.

Canada (*see* also Ontario and British Columbia), legislative control in, 103; term of municipal councillors in, 161; enumeration of municipal powers in, 171; election of mayors in, 181.

Cemeteries, municipal, 30.

Central control over municipal authorities, 12, 13; necessity of, 69, 70, 71; nature of problems of, 72, 113; sphere of control, 92-102; area and boundaries of corporation, 93-96; police administration, 96, 97; public health, 97, 98; administration of justice, 98, 99; public charity, 99, 100; public education, 100, 101; finance, 101, 102; methods of control, 102-114; legislative control, 103, 104; judicial control, 104; administrative control, 105-114.

Centralization of responsibility in American municipal government, 227-231.

Charters of cities, framing of, by local representatives, 84-87.

Chemnitz, technical schools of, 48.

Chicago, local divisions of, and assessment of property in, 7, 8; area, 8; special constitutional provisions for, 91; percentage of foreign-born in, 118; size of council of, 161; council committees of, 167; mayor president of council in, 170; term of mayor of, 183; mayor in charge of police of, 189; salary of mayor of, 191; civil service reform in, 207-209; jury problem in, 226; condition of home life in, 239.

Cincinnati, railroad built by, 42; board of legislation committee on "general assembly," 67; police board, 97; inequality of wards in, 136; committees of council of, 166; salaries of councillors, 178; mayor a member of police board of, 189; board of administration of, 197; boards of, appointed by the governor, 199; bipartisan system in, 205.

Cincinnati Southern Railroad, a municipal undertaking, 42.

Citizenship, a qualification for suffrage, 118-120.

City, a state, 73-78; in constitutional law, 78-91; a creature and agent of government, 91-114; isolation of, 235, 236.

City-state, forms of, 73-78; absolutely independent, 74; in dependent alliance, 74, 75; the feudal city, 75-78; in federal government, 78.

City courts, criminal jurisdiction of, 32, 33; organization of, 214, 227.

City judiciary, 214-227; organization of, 214; corporation courts, 214-216; local courts of general system, 216-220; appointment and tenure of judicial officers, 220, 221; judicial procedure, 221-223; ministerial functions of the judiciary, 223, 224; public prosecution, 224, 225; jury system, 225-227.

City magistrates, summary jurisdiction of, 34.

Civil service in cities, 206-209.

Civil service reform, 207-209.

Civilization, the progress of, as related to city conditions, 240-242.

Class representation, 157.

Classification of functions, external and internal, 16; primary and secondary, 22, 52; protective and socialistic, 36, 37.

Cleveland, size of city council of, 161, 162; term of mayor of, 183; department of public works in, 195; cabinet system in government of, 196; term of department heads in, 201; school government of, 203.

Clignancourt, quarter of Paris, population of, 138.

Coining money, a function of government, 38.

Collections, museums, gardens, fairs, etc., maintained by cities, 49.

Colorado, special municipal commissions in, 83; woman suffrage in, 123; size of legislature of, 163.

Conditions of city life, 4, 5, 43; their effect upon political capacity, 236-238; social disintegration in cities, 238-240.

Congestion in city life, 4.

Connecticut, state enforcement of school attendance law in, 101.

Constables, 26, 27, 223.

Constitutional law, the city established in, 78-91; in national constitutions, 79; in commonwealth constitutions, 79-91; local choice of local officers guaranteed, 81-84; formation of charters by city itself guaranteed, 84-87; special legislation prohibited, 87-89; limitation of city's financial powers, 89, 90; special provisions, 90, 91.

Contracts, public, analogy from, 22.

Control over government, sources of, 72, 73. (*See also* Central Control.)

Copenhagen, appointment of chief executives of, 182.

Corporation courts, 214-216.

Corporations, creation of, by government, 41, 42.

Council, municipal, 143-179; importance of, 143-148; qualifications of members of, 148, 149; election areas, 150, 151; principle of representation, 151, 152; minority representation, 152-156; proportional representation, 156, 157; class representation, 157; methods of nomination, 157-160; term of service, 160, 161; size of council, 162-163; organization into chambers, 163-165; methods of procedure, 165-167; sessions of council, 167, 168; powers of council, 168; over its own organization, 169, 170; general legislative powers, 170-173; corporate powers, 173, 174; powers of direct administration, 174; judicial powers, 174, 175; powers of control over municipal officers, 175, 176, duties, limitations, emoluments, etc., of councilmen, 176-178.

County officers, removal of, in New York, 106.

Courts, civil, protection of rights by, 33.

Crematory, municipal, in Paris, 30.

Cumulative voting, 155, 156.

Defective and dependent classes, care of, 34-36; relief of the poor, 34, 35; the insane and idiots, 35; the blind, deaf, etc., 35; orphans and outcasts, 36.

Delaware, size of legislature of, 162.

Delian confederacy, Athenian influence in, 75.

Democracy, and private interests of government, 23; test of, in cities, 238, 240-243.

Denmark, appointment of mayors in, 182.

Denver, salary of mayor of, 191; boards of, appointed by the governor, 199; bipartisan system in, 205.

Depots and warehouses, maintained by government, 45.

Detroit, potato farms in, 40; electric lighting, 47; police board, 1865, 97; health board appointed by governor, 98; election by general ticket in, 150; compulsory official service in, 179; term of mayor of, 183; boards of, appointed by the governor, 199.

Disease, prevention and suppression of, 28, 29.

Disqualifications for suffrage, 133, 134.

Distribution of governmental functions, a problem of political science, 69.

Distribution of information, a function of government, 39.

Districts of the city, 134-143.

Division of the city into districts, 134-143; electoral districts, 134-138; administrative districts, 138-141; principles governing the division into districts, 141-143.

Docks and wharves, maintained or regulated by cities, 45.

Domestic necessities, distribution of, by government, 46, 47.

Dublin, model tenements, 30; number of municipal voters in, 125; honorary freedom of the city, 133; council committees in, 167.

Dundee, Scotland, city churches, 17; freedom of the city, 18, 133; mortification grants in trust, 58.

Economic activity, promotion of, by city government, 37 *et seq.*

Economic condition, a qualification for suffrage, 124, 125.

Ecuador, municipal self-government in, 79.

Education, a qualification for suffrage, 129, 130.

Election areas, for councilmen, 150, 151.
Elections, purpose of, 22; provided for by government, 65, 66.
Electoral districts in cities, 134–138.
Electorate, the municipal, 117–134; qualifications for suffrage, citizenship, 118–120; residence, 120–122; age, 122; sex, 122–124; economic condition, 124, 125; tax-paying, 125–129; family condition, 129; education, 129, 130; membership in extra-governmental organizations, 131, 132; municipal freedom, 132, 133; disqualifications for suffrage, 133, 134.
Electric lighting works, maintained by cities, 46, 47.
Empire city, ancient, basis for modern national state, 74; obverse of municipal corporation, 92.
England (*see also* Great Britain and British Empire), criminal jurisdiction of boroughs in, 12, 13; public schools in, 48; borough elections in, 65; optional municipal acts, 66; central control in, 70; feudal cities of, in middle ages, 76, 77, 78; incorporation of cities in, 94; control of police in, 97; control over sanitary administration in, 98; central control over poor relief in, 99; central control over schools in, 100; central control over finances of cities, 102; legislative control in, 103; judicial control in, 104; administrative control in, 105, 108; control over municipal by-laws, 109; grant of financial aid to municipalities in, 111; residence qualification for suffrage, 120; woman suffrage in, 123; lodgers' franchise, 125; effect of tax-paying qualification in, 128, 129; householder's qualification in, 129; poor relief and suffrage in, 134; municipal council in, 143, 144; residence of borough councillors in, 149; general representation in, 152; cumulative voting in, 155, 156; method of nominations for municipal councillors in, 157, 158; term of municipal councillors in, 161; aldermen in municipal councils of, 164; administrative powers of councillors in, 174; compulsory official service in, 178; unsalaried municipal councillors in, 179; position of mayors in, 181; term of mayors in, 183, 184; mayor a justice of the peace in, 188; privileges of the mayoralty in, 190; administrative unity in cities of, 198; councils' appointing power in, 198; term of municipal department heads in, 201, 202; municipal boards in, 202; council committees subject to councils in, 211; municipal courts in, 215; independence of the judiciary in, 220; stipendiary magistrates and recorders in boroughs of, 220; constables in, 223; council system in, 230.
Entrepots, of Paris, 45.
Essen, Germany, electors in, 127.
Europe, municipal property as source of revenue in, 55; central control over cities, 70; feudal dependence of mediæval cities in, 75; administrative control in, 105, 108; protection of individual rights in, 110; municipal council in, 143; size of municipal councils in, 161; mayor as president of municipal councils in, 170; general grant of mu-

nicipal powers in, 172; election of mayors in, 182; administrative unity in cities of, 197; contribution of the sciences to municipal government in, 213; experience of, opposed to one-man power in city government, 230.

Evarts, Hon. W. M., commission to devise plan for city government in New York state, 126.

Excise taxes and licenses, revenue from, in New York city, 61.

Family, the, its influence on morals, 51, 52; disintegration of, in cities, 238, 239.

Family condition, a qualification for suffrage, 129.

Fascination of city life, 4.

Federal government, membership of the city in, 78.

Feudal cities, military organization of, 25; degree of independence of, 75-78.

Financial aid to localities a means of central control, 111-113.

Financial powers of cities, limitation of, by constitutional provisions, 89, 90; subject to central supervision, 101, 102.

Fire, protection against, 27.

Florence, independence of, in the middle ages, 76.

Florida, special municipal legislation in, 88; removal of local officers, 106.

Food inspection, a function of city government, 62, 63.

Foreign affairs, as a function of city government, 17-19.

France, municipal street-car system in, 45; octroi taxes, 58; municipal food inspection, 63; civil liberty in mediæval communes of, 71; feudal cities of, in middle ages, 76; formation of new communes in, 94; control of police in, 97; control of municipal health administration in, 97; central control over poor relief, 99; central control over schools in, 100; centralization of financial administration in, 101, 102; removal of mayors in, 107; control over municipal by-laws, 108, 109; administrative courts in, 110; municipal autonomy in, 114; communal suffrage, 120; residence qualification in, 121; age qualification in, 122; municipal council in, 146; non-resident municipal councillors in, 149; election of municipal councils in, 150; nominations for municipal councillors in, 157; term of municipal councillors in, 161; sessions of municipal councils in, 167; municipal budgets in, 177; unsalaried municipal councillors in, 179; importance of *maires* in, 180; term of mayors in, 184; position of mayors in, 184; mayors prepare municipal budgets in, 186; mayor's powers in communes of, 188, 189; privileges of the mayoralty in, 190, 191; administrative unity in cities of, 197; mayor's appointing power in, 198; term of municipal adjuncts in, 202; municipal civil service examinations in, 209; department chiefs responsible to mayors in, 211; limitation of mayor's power in, 230.

Freedom, municipal, a qualification for suffrage, 132, 133.

Functions of city government, problems of, 12, 13; relation of political science to, 14-16; external functions, 16-19; religion, 16, 17; foreign affairs, 17, 19;

primary and secondary, distinguished, 21-24; primary, 24-52; public safety, 24-27; against armies and mobs, 25, 26; against criminals, 26, 27; against fire, flood, and wind, 27; public health, 28-32; administration of justice, 32-34; prosecution of criminals, 32, 33; protection of rights, 33; enforcement of police regulations, 33, 34; care of defective and dependent classes, 34-36; paupers, 34, 35; insane and idiotic, 35; physical defectives, 35; orphans and outcast children, 36; protective and socialistic functions distinguished, 36, 37; promotion of economic activity and thrift, 37-42; coinage, 38; banks and pawnshops, 38; protection of industry, 38, 39; distribution of information, 39; self-help, 39, 40; levelling up industrial depressions, 40, 41; establishment of corporations, 41, 42; preservation of natural resources, 42; making of internal improvements, 42; rendering of common public services, 43-47; transportation, 43-45; maintenance of terminals, 45; public institutions for common service, 46; distribution of domestic necessities, 46, 47; water and electric power, 47; idealistic functions, 47, 48; encouragement of public education, 48-50; public schools, 48; public libraries, 49; collections, 49; exhibitions, 49, 50; promotion of public morality, 50-52; teaching of good citizenship, 51; suppression of vice, 51; reformation of delinquents, 51; maintenance of a code of law, 51, 52; secondary functions, 52-69; raising of revenue, 53-61; by management of property, 54-56; by loans, 56, 57; by gifts and legacies, 57, 58; by taxation, 58, 59; by police regulation, 59-61; maintenance of public works, 61, 62; public buildings, 61; public plants, 62; making of public inspection, 62-64; statistics, 62; inspection of food, 62, 63; building inspection, 63; inspection of institutions, 63; governmental self-inspection, 63; provision for expression of the public will, 64-67; elections, 65, 66; referendum, 66; popular initiative, 66, 67; representation of the citizens in their corporate capacity, 67-69; before the legislature, 67, 68; before the central administrative authorities, 68; with other municipal corporations, 68; in the courts, 68, 69; distribution of functions between central and local governments, 69-71.

Gas works, maintained by cities, 46, 47.
Geneva, Swiss canton, mayor's position in communes of, 188.
Genoa, independence of, in the middle ages, 76.
Georgia, size of legislature of, 162.
Germany (*see also* Prussia), municipal lighting plants in, 47; municipal street franchises, 60; municipal food inspection, 63; control over municipal by-laws in, 109; administrative courts in, 110; municipal autonomy in, 114; municipal council in, 144, 146, 163; joint standing committees in municipal councils of, 165; sessions of municipal councils in, 168; administrative

powers of municipal councillors in, 174; municipal budgets in, 177; importance of *bürgermeister* in, 180, 181; approval of appointment of burgomasters in, 182; term of mayors in, 184; municipal executive's veto power in, 186; administrative powers of burgomasters in, 190; salaries of burgomasters in, 191; administrative unity in cities of, 197; council's appointing power in, 198; term of municipal staff officers in, 202; municipal commissions in, 202; municipal civil service examinations in, 209; legislative powers of municipal administrative departments in, 211; board system used in, 230.

Gifts and legacies, municipal, a source of revenue, 57, 58.

Glasgow, area, 8; public reception, 18; tenements and lodging houses, 30; relief works in, 41; improvement of the Clyde, 42; technical schools, 48; free libraries act rejected, 49, 66; municipal concerts in, 50; municipal property and tax rate, 55; expansion of territory of, 95, 96; freedom of the city, 133; nominating system in, 158; size of council of, 161; public prosecutor in, 225.

Grand Rapids, council committees in, 166, 167; salaries of aldermen in, 178; marshal's term in, 224.

Great Britain (*see also* England and British Empire), municipal street-car transportation, 45; municipal lighting plants, 47; free municipal libraries, 49; municipal property in, 55; municipal street franchises, 60; municipal food inspection, 63; increase of municipal independence in, 114; nominating system in, 158; election of mayors in, 182.

Greater New York, area, 8; framing of charter, 86; creation of, 96; removal of mayor, 106; civil divisions of, 142, 143; size of council of, 162; bicameral system in, 163; special majorities required by charter of, 165, 166; powers of council over its own organization in, 169; president of council in, 170; enumeration of powers in charter of, 171, 172; salaries of councillors, 178; position of mayor of, 185; term of mayor of, 183; mayor's legislative powers in, 187, 188; salary of mayor of, 191; administrative departments in, 194; board of public improvements in, 195, 197; appointment of city clerk in, 199; term of department heads in, 201; organization of department heads in, 202, 203; marshals in, 224; budge of, 235.

Greater Republic of Central America, 80.

Greece, ancient, municipal theatrical entertainments in, 49.

Hamburg, in the German Empire, 17, 18; effect of tax-paying qualifications in, 128, 129; corporate bodies and the suffrage in, 131, 132, 156; term of municipal councillors in, 161.

Hanover, technical schools of, 48.

Hartford, term of mayor under early charter of, 183.

Hawaiian Republic, no system of municipal government in, 92, 93.

Head of the corporation, 179-191. (*See also* Mayor.)

Health, protection of public, 28–

S

32; by prevention and suppression of disease, 28, 29; by disposal of refuse, 29, 30; by removal of the dead, 30; by provision of housing, 30; by provision of light, air, and room, 31; by provision of food-supply, 31, 32; administration of public health under central control, 97, 98.

Hearings, public, as a means for expressing the people's will, 66.

Holland (*see also* The Netherlands), age qualification for suffrage in, 122; municipal councillors in, 149; term of municipal councillors in, 161; appointment of mayors in, 182.

Honduras, municipal self-government in, 80.

Horse-racing, encouraged by Paris, 50.

Huddersfield, technical schools of, 48.

Hungary, seats in municipal councils in, 148; term of municipal councillors in, 161.

Idaho, general incorporation act required for cities in, 88; municipal indebtedness limited in, 90; woman suffrage in, 123.

Illinois, special municipal legislation prohibited in, 88; municipal indebtedness limited in, 90; school suffrage for women in, 124; cumulative voting in, 155, 156; size of legislature of, 162; municipal incorporations act of, 171.

Indiana, special municipal legislation prohibited in, 88; municipal indebtedness limited in, 90.

Indianapolis, manual training high school of, 48; term of mayor of, 183; municipal departments of, 194; department of public works in, 195.

Industrial depressions, levelled up by governmental action, 40, 41.

Initiative, popular, as a means of expressing the public will, 66.

Insane, care of the, 35.

Inspection, public, 22, 62–64.

Internal improvements, executed by government, 42.

Iowa, special municipal legislation prohibited in, 88; municipal indebtedness limited in, 90.

Issuance of instructions, a means of central control, 108.

Italy, municipal octroi taxes in, 58; mediæval cities of, 75, 76; age qualification for suffrage in, 122; educational qualification in, 129; term of municipal councillors in, 161; appointment of mayors in, 182; position of mayors in, 184.

Jersey City, term of mayor of, 183.

Judicial control, nature of, 104; methods of, by appeal and by issue of special writs, 104.

Judiciary, organization of municipal, 214–227.

Jury system, problems of, 225, 227.

Justice, administration of, 32–34; prosecution of criminals, 32, 33; protection of rights, 33; enforcement of police regulations, 33, 34; subject to central control, 98, 99.

Kansas, United States Supreme Court decision affecting municipal bonds in state of, 38, 39; special municipal legislation prohibited in, 88; municipal suffrage for women in, 123.

Kansas City, sessions of city council in, 168.

Kentucky, election of local officers

in, 83; special municipal legislation prohibited in, 88; municipal indebtedness and tax rate limited in, 90.

Labor bureau, in New York city, 39.
Labor exchange, established by Paris, 39.
Laboratories, maintained by government, 46.
Legislative control, nature of, 103, 104.
Leopoldstadt, district of Vienna, population of, 139.
Levees and dykes, protection against flood, 27.
Li Hung Chang, received by mayors, 18.
Lille, technical schools of, 48.
Liverpool, model tenements, 30; creation of Greater Liverpool, 96; inequality in wards of, 135, 136.
Loans, municipal, a source of revenue, 56, 57.
Local government, neglect of problem, 1, 3; uniformity of, destroyed by cities, 6–9.
Local self-government, struggle for, 2; problem of, 3; back of written constitutions, 20, 21; guaranteed by constitutional provisions, 78, 79.
Lodging houses, public, 46.
Lombard League, rights of cities under, 75, 76, 98.
London, city of, public receptions, 18; military of, 25; power of, over Thames fisheries, 42; diversion of endowment funds, 57; jurisdiction of courts of, 98, 99; guild organizations and the suffrage in, 131; wards of, 135; population of, 138; courts of, 215.
London, county of, local divisions, 7; area, 8; docks in, 45; tax reform in, 59; police in, 96; percentage of foreign-born in, 118; electoral divisions of, 138; local authorities and elections in, 139, 140; local divisions of, 142; term of county councillors of, 161; size of council, 161.
Louisiana, framing of city charters in, 87; special municipal legislation prohibited in, 88; citizenship in, 149.
Louisville, election of aldermen by general ticket in, 151; term of mayor of, 183.
Lübeck, in the German Empire, 17, 78.
Lynn, joint standing committees of council of, 165; other committees, 166.

Maine, municipal indebtedness limited in, 89.
Manchester, ship canal, 42; rent of gas stoves by, 47; industrial power furnished by, 47; technical schools, 48; council sub-committee on parliamentary matters, 67; size of council of, 161; council committees in, 167, 195, 196.
Manhattan, borough of Greater New York, 142.
Manhattan Island, wards of New York city on, 140.
Manufactures, assistance of, by cities, 38, 39.
Markets, maintained by cities, 45.
Marseilles, technical schools of, 48.
Marshals, 26, 223, 224.
Massachusetts, state charities board in, 100; school suffrage for women in, 124; educational qualification in, 130; size of legislature of, 162; competitive civil service examinations in, 207.

Mayor, or head of the municipal corporation, 179-191; importance of, 179-181; how chosen, 181, 182; term of service, 182-184; official position, 184; legislative powers, 184-188; judicial powers, 188; administrative powers, 188-190; privileges and emoluments of the mayoralty, 190, 191.

McDonough grant to Baltimore and New Orleans, 57.

Mediæval cities, 1.

Membership in extra-governmental organizations, a qualification for suffrage, 131, 132.

Memphis, Tennessee, legislative council of, 164; mayor of, 181, 182.

Michigan, local self-government in the choice of local officers in, 82; removal of local officers in, 106, 107; school suffrage for women in, 124; size of legislature of, 162; removal of mayors in, 184; bipartisan system unconstitutional in, 205.

Milan, technical schools of, 48; in mediæval times, 75.

Military organization of cities, 25, 26.

Milwaukee, term of mayor of, 183; civil service reform in, 207.

Minneapolis, council government in, 147; term of mayor of, 183; mayor in control of police of, 189; salary of mayor of, 191; appointing power of council in, 198.

Minnesota, framing of city charters in, 86, 87; special municipal legislation prohibited in, 88; removal of county treasurers, 106; school suffrage for women in, 124.

Minority representation, 152-156.

Mississippi, special municipal legislation prohibited in, 88; educational qualification in, 130.

Mississippi River, levees, 27.

Missouri, framing of city charters in, 84; special municipal legislation prohibited in, 88; municipal indebtedness limited in, 89; municipal tax rate limited in, 90.

Modern city, 4-6.

Montana, special municipal commissions in, 83; municipal indebtedness limited in, 90.

Morality, public, promotion of, by government, 50-52; teaching of good citizenship, 51; suppression of vice, 51; maintenance of reformatories, 51; maintenance of a code of law, 51, 52.

Municipal corporation, the city as a, 74, 91, 92.

Musical and theatrical exhibitions, furnished by cities, 49, 50.

Natural resources, preservation of, by government, 42.

Nebraska, special municipal legislation prohibited in, 88.

Netherlands, The (*see also* Holland), municipal self-government in, 79.

Nevada, general incorporation act required for cities in, 88; size of legislature of, 163.

Newark, term of mayor of, 183.

New Bedford, term of mayor of, 183.

Newcastle-on-Tyne, municipal concerts in, 50.

New England, mayor president of upper chamber of municipal councils in, 170; terms of mayors in cities of, 182, 183.

New Hampshire, size of legislature of, 163.

New Haven, joint standing committees of council of, 165; term of mayor of, 183.

New Jersey, special municipal legislation prohibited in, 88; incorporation of new municipalities in, 94.

New Orleans, the McDonough grant, 57; special legislation for, allowed, 88; special constitutional provisions for, 90; administrative system of government tried in, 147, 148; pay of councillors in, 178; term of mayor in, 183; mayor's veto power in, 185; salary of mayor of, 191; administrative unity in government of, 197; boards of, appointed by the governor, 199; civil service reform in, 207; election of recorders in, 221.

New South Wales (*see also* Australia), central control over municipal finances in, 102; control over municipal by-laws, 109; subsidies to municipalities in, 111; citizenship not required for suffrage in, 123; woman suffrage in, 123; rate-paying qualification in, 128; non-resident municipal councillors in, 149; nominating system in, 158, 159.

New York city (*see* Greater New York), area, 8; tenth ward, area and population, 8; public receptions, 18; bounties to soldiers, and armories, 26; health board, 29; rear tenements, 30; state labor bureau in, 39; royalties under old charters, 42; docks in, 45; Croton water supply, 46; nautical school, 48; public library, 49; tax-levying by, 55; municipal property, 56; loans in 1896, 57; special assessments in, 59; revenue from franchises, 60; excise revenues, 61; buildings department of, 63; election of department heads, 65; vote on consolidation, 66; policy of corporation counsel toward legislation, 68; Brooklyn bridge, 68; charter conventions, 84, 85; special constitutional provisions for, 90; metropolitan police board of, 97, 199; metropolitan fire board, 97; metropolitan health board, 98; corporation courts abolished, 98; removal of mayor, 106, 184; municipal ordinances of, under early charters, 109; political campaign of 1894 in, 116; percentage of foreign-born in, 118; corrupt naturalization in, 119; shifting of the population, 121, 122; school officers appointed in, 124; former qualifications for municipal suffrage in, 124, 125; hearings on the budget of, 126; "freedom" and the royal charters of, 132; electoral divisions of, 137; wards of, 140; administrative divisions of, 141; common council of, 147; minority representation in, 152, 155; size of council, 161; board of estimate, 162, 196; assistant aldermen in early council of, 164; separation of powers in charter of 1830 of, 164, 165; council committees in, 167; president of board of aldermen in, 170; budget of, 173; administrative powers of aldermen under old charters of, 174; judicial powers of first council of, 174; compulsory official service in, 179; mayor's legislative powers in, 186, 187; salary of mayor of, 191; change in methods of appointing boards of, 199, 200; election of department heads in, 200, 201; term of department heads in, 201;

bipartisan system in, 204, 205; internal organization in charters of, 206; legislative powers of administrative departments of, 209, 210; street-cleaning department of, under Colonel Waring, 212, 213; police judges of, 216; municipal courts of, 217-219; appointment, election, and terms of judges in, 221; board of city magistrates in, 223; marshal's duties in, 223; public administration in, 224; public prosecution in, under Tammany rule, 225; jury exemptions in, 226; jury problem in, 226; commissioner of jurors in, 227; conditions of home life in, 239.

New York county, district attorney in, 225.

New York state, public hearings on municipal legislation in, 66; election of local officers in, 81, 82; city conventions in, 84-86; special municipal legislation in, 88, 89; municipal indebtedness limited in, 89; municipal tax rate limited in, 90; state charities board, 100; governor's power of removal over local officers, 106; civil service board, 108; school suffrage for women in, 124; size of legislature, 162; mayors in, 182; government of cities of second class in, 185, 186; mayor's suspensive veto power in cities of, 186; bipartisan system unconstitutional in, 205, 206; detailed provision for organization of cities in, 206; competitive civil service examinations in, 207; Governor Black's scheme in, 208, 209; budget of, 235.

New Zealand, woman suffrage in, 123.

Nomination, methods of, 157-160.

North Dakota, special municipal legislation prohibited in, 88; municipal indebtedness limited in, 90; size of legislature of, 162.

Nottingham, technical schools of, 48.

Odessa, municipal theatre in, 50.

Officers, local choice of, in New York, 81, 82; in Michigan, 82; in other commonwealths, 83; appointment and removal of, 105-108.

Ohio, municipal aid to manufactures authorized in, 39; special municipal legislation prohibited in, 88; new municipal corporations in, 94, 95; state charities board, 100; state control over local finances in, 102; school suffrage for women in, 124.

Oldham, technical schools of, 48.

Omaha, election of councillors by general ticket, 151; term of mayors in, 183; boards of, appointed by the governor, 199.

Ontario (*see also* Canada), municipal residence required for suffrage, 121; woman suffrage in, 123; nominating system in, 158-160; enumeration of municipal powers in, 171.

Ordinances, general police, 33, 34.

Organization, problems of, 12, 13, 115-233; local importance of, 115-117; the electorate, 117-134; divisions of the city into districts, 134-143; the council, 143-179; the head of the corporation, 179-191; the administrative departments, 191-214; the city judiciary, 214-227; meaning of organization, 227-233.

Orphans and outcast children, care of, 36.

Paris, population and area, 8; municipal crematory, 30; municipal pawnshops and savings banks, 38; labor exchange established by, 39; *entrepots* in, 45; technical schools, 48; municipal theatres and horse-racing, 50; municipal debt, 57; revenue from street franchises, 60; police in, 96; percentage of foreign-born in, 118; electoral divisions of, 137, 138; arrondissements of, 138, 139; local divisions of, 142; size of council, 161; council committees in, 167; police department in, 196; police commissaries in, 216; budget of, 235.

Parks, boulevards, and playgrounds, provision of, by cities, 31.

Pawnshops, maintenance or regulation of, a function of government, 38.

Pawtucket, joint standing committees of council of, 165; appointing power of council in, 198.

Peace of Constance, effect of, upon independence of Italian cities, 75, 76.

Pennsylvania, special municipal commissions in, 83; special municipal legislation prohibited in, 88; municipal indebtedness limited in, 90; removal of local officers, 106; size of legislature, 162; enumeration of municipal powers in, 171; act relating to Philadelphia by legislature of, 200.

Petitions, public, as a means of expressing the people's will, 66.

Philadelphia, area, 8; public reception, 18, municipal ownership of gas, 47; revenue from street-car franchises, 60, 61; percentage of foreign-born in, 118; board of public education, 124; representation of wards in common council of, 135; size of council, 161; bicameral council in, 163; joint standing committees of councils of, 165; council committees in, 167; judicial powers of aldermen in, 174, 175; term of mayor of, 183; salary of mayor of, 191; department of public safety in, 193; department of public works, 195; confirmation of mayor's nominations by council of, 200; conditions of home life in, 239.

Physical defectives, care of, 35.

Physical force, basis of sovereignty, 24, 25.

Pittsburg, joint standing committees of council of, 165; salary of mayor of, 191; administrative departments of, 193; department of public works in, 195.

"Plants," municipal, establishment of, 62.

Police, military functions, 25; ministerial functions to the judiciary, 26, 223; as state officers, 27; subject to central control, 96, 97.

Police justices, summary jurisdiction of, 34.

Police ordinances, important in cities, 33.

Police regulation, municipal, a source of revenue, 59-61.

Political capacity, effect of city life upon, 236-238.

Political economy, relation of, to governmental functions, 14, 15.

Political parties, in municipal elections, 19; represented on municipal boards, 203-206.

Political science, unit of, 1; relation

of, to governmental functions, 14-16; science of method, 24.
Poor relief, 34, 35; subject to central control, 99, 100.
Portland, Me., term of mayor of, 183.
Position of the city, unity with general government, 10; as agent of state, 11; as a social fact, 11; as a corporation, 11.
"Potato-patch" scheme, in Detroit and Buffalo, 40.
Poughkeepsie, removal of mayor, 106.
Power furnished to factories by cities, 47.
Powers of municipal councils, 168-176; of internal organization, 169, 170; legislative, 170-173; corporate, 173, 174; of direct administration, 174; judicial, 174, 175; of control, 175, 176.
Primary functions, 24-52. (*See* Functions, primary.)
Prison wardens, 26.
Prisons, centralization of administration, 26.
Problems of city government, classification of, 12; problems of function, 14-71; problems of control, 72-114; problems of organization, 115-233; summary of, 242, 243.
Procedure of municipal council, methods of, 165-167; judicial, 221-223.
Property, municipal, a source of revenue, 54-56.
Proportional representation, 156, 157.
Prostitution, suppression of, by public authorities, 50, 51.
Protection of industry, a function of government, 38.
Protective functions of government, 36, 37.

Providence, size of city council of, 161; joint standing committees of council of, 165; term of mayor of, 183.
Provost, Lord, ceremonial functions in Scotch cities, 18.
Prussia (*see also* Germany), municipal elections, 65; central control of police in, 96; central control over municipal finances, 102; appointment of burgomasters in, 108; municipal ordinances in, 109; superior administrative court of, 110; age qualification for suffrage in, classes of electors in, 127, 157; effect of tax-paying qualification in, 129; compulsory official service in, 179; unsalaried municipal councillors in, 179; town executive's veto power in, 186; cities of the twelfth century in, 217.
Public administrator, in cities, 224.
Public buildings, purpose of, 21; maintenance of, by government, 61.
Public charities, subject to central control, 99, 100.
Public education, a function of government, 48-50; subject to central control, 100, 101.
Public libraries, maintained by cities, 49.
Public prosecution, 224, 225.
Public works, maintenance of, a secondary function of government, 61, 62.

Quebec, municipal council of, 182.
Queens, borough of Greater New York, 142.

Raines excise law, 61.
Reading, term of mayor of, 183.

Reception of visitors by cities, Li Hung Chang, 18; at Grant monument dedication, 18; in Great Britain, 18.

Recreation, means of, not furnished for its own sake, 31.

Referendum, as a means of testing the public will, 66.

Reform in municipal government, its fitfulness, 9.

Refuse, disposal of, 29, 30.

Rejection of local by-laws and projects, a means of central control, 108–110.

Religion, as a function of city government, 16, 17.

Removal of city officers, a means of central control, 105, 108.

Representation principles of, 151–157; locality, 152; minority, 152–156; proportional, 156, 157; class, 157.

Residence, a qualification for suffrage, 120–122.

Revenue, municipal, purpose of raising, 20; as illustration, 24; from what sources derived, 54–61.

Rhode Island, size of legislature of, 162.

Richmond, borough of Greater New York, 142.

Richmond, city, term of mayor of, 183.

Rochester, special constitutional provision for, 91 n.; council government in, 147; council committees in, 167; compulsory official service in, 179; municipal court of, 216.

Roman Empire, central control over municipal finances in, 101, 105.

Rome, ancient, influence on city-state, 1; public religious ceremonies, 16; an independent state, 74; control over other cities, 75; relation of, to the empire, 92.

St. Louis, cyclone of 1896, 27; special constitutional provisions for, 90; police board, 97; freehold qualification for councilmen, 124; election of council by general ticket in, 150; size of council, 161; bicameral council in, 163; term of mayor of, 183; mayor a member of the police board of, 189; salary of mayor of, 191; board of public improvements in, 195; boards of, appointed by the governor, 199.

Salisbury, municipal treaty formed by, 77.

Salt Lake City, term of mayor of, 183; appointing power of council in, 198; police justice of, 215.

San Francisco, water supply, 46; elections in, 65; charter of, 86; percentage of foreign-born in, 118; council and school board of, 151; size of council of, 161; council committees in, 167; mayor president of the council in, 170; salary of mayor of, 191; boards of, appointed by the governor, 199; proposed civil service reform in, 207; public administrator in, 224; jury problem in, 226.

Santé, quarter of Paris, population of, 137.

Scotland (*see also* Great Britain), gas stoves rented by cities, 47; municipal nominations in royal burghs of, 158, 159.

Scranton, term of mayor of, 183.

Seattle, term of mayor of, 183.

Self-help, opportunities for, furnished by government, 39, 40.

GENERAL INDEX.

Separation of executive and administrative functions, 191, 192.
Sessions of municipal councils, 167, 168.
Sewage, disposal of, 29, 30, 52.
Sex, a qualification for suffrage, 122, 124.
Sheriffs, 26, 223.
Ship canal, constructed by Manchester, 42.
Simmering, district of Vienna, population of, 139.
Size of council, 161–163.
Slaughter-houses, public, 46. [240.
Social disintegration in cities, 238–
Socialism, and business in city government, 20.
Socialistic functions of government, 36 et seq.
Sociology, relation of, to governmental functions, 14–15.
South Carolina, special municipal legislation prohibited in, 88; municipal indebtedness limited in, 90; educational qualification in, 130.
South Dakota, special municipal legislation prohibited in, 88; municipal indebtedness limited in, 90.
Southampton, municipal treaties formed by, 77.
Sovereignty, based on might, 25.
Spain, municipal residence required for suffrage, 121; age qualification in, 122.
Sparta, ancient, an independent state, 74; domination over allied cities, 75.
Special legislation affecting cities, prohibited in many commonwealths, 87–89.
Special writs, issue of, a method of judicial control, 104.
Spoils system, in the United States, 21.
Springfield, Mass., joint standing committees of council of, 165; term of mayor of, 183; police court of, 215, 216; city marshal in, 224.
Statistics, collection of, by government, 62.
Stockholm, tax-paying qualification for suffrage in, 128.
Street railways, maintained or supervised by government, 44, 45; in Philadelphia, 60, 61.
Streets, maintenance of, by government, 43, 44.
Study of the city, 9–12; divisions of the study, 12, 13; study of individual departments, 211–214.
Summary jurisdiction of city authorities, 34.
Superior administrative court of Prussia, 110. [182.
Sweden, appointment of mayors in,
Switzerland, popular initiative in, 66; municipal suffrage in, 121; age qualification in, 122; proportional representation in, 156.
Syracuse, local court in, 221.

Taxation, a source of revenue, 58, 59.
Tax-paying, a qualification for suffrage, 125–129.
Technical schools, maintained by cities, 48.
Tenement houses, construction and regulation of, by cities, 30.
Term of official service, of councillors, 160, 161; of mayor, 182–184; of heads of departments, 201, 202.
Terminals, maintenance of, by government, 45.
Texas, special municipal legislation in, 88; municipal tax rate limited in, 90; size of legislature of, 162.

Thames River, fisheries in, 42.
Theatres, maintained by cities, 49, 50.
Thrift, promotion of, by city government, 37 *et seq.*
Tilden, Governor Samuel J., 126.
Topeka, Kansas, municipal bonds declared illegal, 38.
Toledo, boards of, appointed by the governor, 199.
Toronto, council committee on legislation in, 67; other committees in, 162.
Transportation, effect upon the growth of cities, 4, 5; provision of, by government, 43, 44.

Unit of political interest, 1-3.
United States, municipal street-car system in, 45; outcry against sumptuary legislation in, 50; municipal taxes in southern commonwealths, 58; general property tax in great cities, 58; municipal food inspection, 63; city departments of buildings, 63; elections in middle of this century, 65; voting on municipal debt and taxation in, 66; popular initiative in cities, 66; central control in, 70; prohibition of special municipal legislation in, 87-89; provisions for city government in constitutions, 91; incorporation of cities in, 94; police boards appointed by state authorities in, 97; metropolitan boards of health in, 98; central control over public charity in, 100; central control over schools in, 100, 101; central control over municipal finances in, 102; legislative control in, 103; judicial control in, 104; administrative control in, 105, 113, 114; governor's powers of appointment and removal in, 105; grant of financial aid to municipalities, 111; citizenship as a qualification for the suffrage in, 118; naturalization in, 118, 119; proportion of foreign-born in cities of, 119; age qualification in, 122; woman suffrage in, 123; theory of taxation in, 126; paupers and suffrage in, 134; inequality of wards in cities of, 136, 137; municipal council in, 143, 146-148; citizenship in, 149; residence of elected officers in, 149; election of municipal councillors by general ticket in, 150, 151; effect of single district system in cities of, 151; local representation in, 152; nominations for municipal councillors in, 157; term of municipal councillors in, 161; size of municipal councils in, 161, 162; size of commonwealth legislatures, 162, 163; bicameral system in cities of, 163, 164; appointment of council committees in cities of, 167; sessions of municipal councils in, 168; enumeration of municipal powers in, 170-173; judicial powers of aldermen in, 175; municipal budgets in, 177; power of mayors in, 180; election of mayors in, 181; term of mayors in, 182; veto power of mayors in, 184; mayor's court in cities of, 188; mayor's administrative powers in, 189; salaries of mayors in, 191; separation of powers in, 191, 192; department of public works in cities of, 195; appointment of municipal department heads in, 198-200; term of service of municipal department heads in, 201; municipal boards and single-headed departments in, 202; legislative powers of municipal administrative departments

in, 211; independence of the judiciary in, 220; election of state and local judges in, 221; constables in, 223; public prosecutor in, 224, 225; the jury problem in cities of, 226; centralization of responsibility in municipal government of, 227-233.

Unity of city with general system of government, 234, 235.

Unity in municipal administration, necessity of, 7; how attained, 175, 176, 196-198.

Utah, special municipal legislation prohibited in, 88; municipal indebtedness limited in, 90; woman suffrage in, 23.

Venice, mediæval, prayer at election of doge, 16; an independent state, 74.

Veto power of mayors, 184-188.

Victoria, central control of municipal finances in, 102; control over municipal by-laws, 109; grant of financial aid to municipalities in, 112, 113; citizenship not required for suffrage, 120; woman suffrage in, 123; rate-paying qualification in, 128; non-resident municipal councillors in, 144; nominating system in, 158, 159.

Vienna, electors in, 128; administrative districts in, 139; local divisions of, 142; size of council of, 161.

Virginia, election of local officers in, 83; general incorporation act required for cities in, 88; municipal indebtedness limited in, 90.

Wandsworth, parliamentary borough of London, 138.

Waring, Colonel George E., Jr., street-cleaning commissioner of New York city, 212-214.

Wash-houses, public, 46.

Washington, city of, control of national government over, 3; no popular elections in, 65.

Washington, state, framing of city charters in, 84; special legislation prohibited in, 88; municipal indebtedness limited in, 90; school suffrage for women in, 124.

Water-works, maintained by cities, 46.

West Virginia, special municipal legislation prohibited in, 88; municipal indebtedness limited in, 90.

Wilmington, Del., freehold qualification for councilmen, 124; council committees in, 167; salaries of councillors in, 178; term of mayor of, 183; board of, appointed by state authorities, 199; appointment of municipal judge in, 221.

Winchester, Eng., municipal treaty formed by, 77.

Wisconsin, local election of local officers in, 82, 83; special municipal legislation prohibited in, 88; municipal indebtedness limited in, 90; governor's power of removal of local officers, 106.

Woman suffrage in English-speaking world, 122-124.

Worcester, term of mayor of, 183.

Wyoming, special municipal commissions in, 84; special municipal legislation prohibited in, 88; municipal indebtedness and tax rate limited in, 90; woman suffrage in, 123.

Yonkers, removal of mayor, 106.

Ypsilanti, school elections in, 123.